File on
CHURCHILL

Compiled by Linda Fitzsimmons

Methuen Drama

A Methuen Drama Book

First published in 1989 as a paperback original
by Methuen Drama, Michelin House,
81 Fulham Road, London SW3 6RB
and HEB Inc., 70 Court Street, Portsmouth
New Hampshire 03801, USA

Copyright in the compilation
©1989 by Linda Fitzsimmons
Copyright in the series format
©1989 by Methuen Drama
Copyright in the editorial presentation
©1989 by Simon Trussler

Typeset in 9/10 Times
by L. Anderson Typesetting
Woodchurch, Kent TN26 3TB

Printed in Great Britain by
Richard Clay Ltd, Bungay, Suffolk

British Library Cataloguing in Publication Data

Fitzsimmons, Linda
   File on Churchill — (Writer-files)
   1. Drama in English. Churchill, Caryl
   I. Title   II. Series
   822'.914

   ISBN 0-413-14730-4

Contents

Acknowledgements

My thanks to Caryl Churchill, who gave me
information and help, read the typescript and
approved the quotations attributed to her; to
Stephanie Tanner of Margaret Ramsay Ltd.,
Churchill's agent; to Laura Stevens,
Mike Johnson and Michael Anderson for help
with translations; to Jo Laurie of the Theatre
Museum; to Rachel Koenig, Amelia Kritzer,
Phyllis Randall, Wolfgang Huber, Richard Seyd,
Eirwen Read, Ron Strang and Mark Sinfield.

The theatre is, by its nature, an ephemeral art: yet it is a daunting task to track down the newspaper reviews, or contemporary statements from the writer or her director, which are often all that remain to help us recreate some sense of what a particular production was like. This series is therefore intended to make readily available a selection of the comments that the critics made about the plays of leading modern dramatists at the time of their production — and to trace, too, the course of each writer's own views about his or her work.

In addition to combining a uniquely convenient source of such elusive *documentation*, the 'Writer-Files' series also assembles the *information* necessary for readers to pursue further their interest in a particular writer or work. Variations in quantity between one writer's output and another, differences in temperament which make some readier than others to talk about their work, and the variety of critical response, all mean that the presentation and balance of material shifts between one volume and another: but we have tried to arrive at a format for the series which will nevertheless enable users of one volume readily to find their way around any other.

Section 1, 'A Brief Chronology', provides a quick conspective overview of each playwright's life and career. *Section 2* deals with the plays themselves, arranged chronologically in the order of their composition: information on first performances, major revivals, and publication is followed by a brief synopsis (for quick reference set in slightly larger, italic type), then by a representative selection of the critical response, and of the dramatist's own comments on the play and its theme.

Section 3 offers concise guidance to each writer's work in non-dramatic forms, while *Section 4*, 'The Writer on Her Work', brings together comments from the playwright herself on more general matters of construction, opinion, and artistic development. Finally, *Section 5* provides a bibliographical guide to other primary and secondary sources of further reading, among which full details will be found of works cited elsewhere under short titles, and of collected editions of the plays — but not of individual titles, particulars of which will be found with the other factual data in Section 2.

The 'Writer-Files' hope by striking this kind of balance between information and a wide range of opinion to offer 'companions' to the study of major playwrights in the modern repertoire — not in that dangerous pre-digested fashion which can too readily quench the desire to read the plays themselves, nor so prescriptively as to allow any single line of approach to predominate, but rather to encourage readers to form their own judgements of the plays in a wide-ranging context.

Caryl Churchill is now generally recognized as among the leading dramatists of her generation. She also happens to be a woman — and some of the earlier reviews in this volume predictably marginalize her concerns as 'women's lib' issues. It is perhaps less predictable that these early notices should also reveal a sharp divergence of critical opinion as to whether the characteristic structure of her plays was (to borrow the polarity as it was expressed in two reviews of *Objections to Sex and Violence*) 'unsurpassed' — or 'tediously talkative' and full of 'irrelevancies'. This seeming contradiction, too, may be reconciled by acknowledging that — as Caryl Churchill puts it on page 90 — 'our whole concept of what plays might be' has (certainly since the romantics) been 'defined by men', as to do with 'conflict, and building in a certain way to a climax'. Conversely, then, the 'feminine' quality of her writing may have simply to do with dialectic replacing conflict, and open-endedness being preferred to climax. Both aspects (of sensibility as reflected in structure) have made her responsive to the workshop approach, through which plays are 'possessed' by company as well as by author.

One possible weakness of a method so closely bound up with the circumstances of a play's first production is that it may make subsequent revivals more tricky — as reports here of some later American and German productions perhaps suggest. Yet just as Brecht is perfectly playable outside the Berliner Ensemble, so is Churchill outside Joint Stock — although (without claiming any equivalence of status) it's also true that both playwrights fuse style and structure, content and form, in ways which challenge traditional perceptions of playwriting and acting.

Despite her long apprenticeship in radio playwriting during the 'sixties, it was, then, surely no accident that her historic moment coincided with the rise of feminist consciousness in the early 'seventies. Her first success in the theatre was, appropriately, with *Owners* — to which, in this volume, one critic duly objects that it lacks the 'classical standards' of 'unity of action and unity of tone'. Yet are these standards really classical — or just masculine? What is refreshing in Churchill's approach to playwriting is her awareness of the fragmentary quality yet essential wholeness of life — and her rendering of it through those sudden, slanting shifts of perception that characterize such plays as *Vinegar Tom*, *Cloud Nine*, *Top Girls*, and *Fen*. Advisedly, Caryl Churchill sacrifices 'unity of action and 'unity of tone' in her recognition of the many-sided cussedness of human action and response.

Simon Trussler

1938 Born in London, 3 September.

1948 Family moved to Montreal, Canada.

1948-55 At the Trafalgar School, Montreal, Canada.

1957-60 At Lady Margaret Hall, Oxford, graduating with B.A. in English Language and Literature. Awarded the Richard Hillary Memorial Prize.

1958 Wrote *Downstairs*, staged by Oriel College Dramatic Society.

1959 *Downstairs* performed at National Union of Students/*Sunday Times* Student Drama Festival. Wrote *You've No Need to be Frightened* and *Having a Wonderful Time*.

1960 Wrote *Easy Death. Having a Wonderful Time* staged at Questors Th., student production.

1961 Wrote *The Ants* and *The Finnsburgh Fragment. Easy Death* staged at Oxford Playhouse, by Oxford Experimental Th. Club, student production. Married David Harter.

1962 *The Ants* broadcast.

1963 First son born.

1964 Second son born.

1965 Wrote *Lovesick.*

1966 *Lovesick* broadcast.

1968 Wrote *Abortive* and *The Marriage of Toby's Idea of Angela and Toby's Idea of Angela's Idea of Toby. Identical Twins* broadcast.

1969 Third son born.

1971 Wrote *Henry's Past* and *The Judge's Wife. Abortive* and *Not ... Not ... Not ... Not ... Not Enough Oxygen* broadcast.

1972 *Schreber's Nervous Illness* and *Henry's Past* broadcast, *The Judge's Wife* on television, *Owners* written and staged at Royal Court Th. Upstairs.

1973 Wrote *Moving Clocks Go Slow, Turkish Delight*, and *Perfect Happiness. Perfect Happiness* broadcast. *Owners* staged at Mercer-Shaw Th., New York.

1974 Wrote *Objections to Sex and Violence. Turkish Delight* on television. Resident dramatist at the Royal Court Th. for a year from autumn 1974.

1975 *Objections to Sex and Violence* staged at Royal Court. *Perfect Happiness* staged at Soho Poly. *Moving Clocks Go Slow* staged at Royal Court Th. Upstairs. Founder-member of Theatre Writers' Group, later Theatre Writers' Union.

1976 Wrote *Traps* and *Vinegar Tom*. Wrote *Light Shining in Buckinghamshire* after workshop with Joint Stock Theatre Group. *Vinegar Tom* staged by Monstrous Regiment, and *Light Shining in Buckinghamshire* staged by Joint Stock.

1977 *Traps* staged at Royal Court Th. Upstairs. Contributed to a cabaret, *Floorshow*, staged by Monstrous Regiment at Th. Royal, Stratford East. Wrote *The After Dinner Joke*. *Objections to Sex and Violence* premiered in Austria (Theater der Courage, Vienna).

1978 Adapted *The Legion Hall Bombing* from Diplock Court trial transcript. Wrote *Softcops*. Wrote *Cloud Nine* after workshop with Joint Stock. *The After Dinner Joke* on television. *Traps* premiered in West Germany (Theater Erlangen).

1979 *The Legion Hall Bombing* on television: Churchill and the director, Roland Joffe, withdrew their names from the credits in protest at censorship by the BBC. *Cloud Nine* staged by Joint Stock. Wrote *Three More Sleepless Nights*.

1980 *Three More Sleepless Nights* staged at Soho Poly. Tutor to Royal Court Young Writers' Group.

1980-82 Wrote *Top Girls*.

1981 *Crimes* written and transmitted on television. *Cloud Nine's* American premiere (Lucille Lortel's Th. de Lys, New York) and Australian premiere (Nimrod Th., Sydney).

1982 *Top Girls* staged at Royal Court and transferred later that year to Joseph Papp's Public Th., New York, presented by the New York Shakespeare Festival. Wrote *Fen* after workshop with Joint Stock. Won OBIE for *Cloud Nine*. *Cloud Nine* premiered in New Zealand (Fortune Th., Dunedin), Japan (Parco Th., Tokyo), Denmark (Det Ny Theater, Copenhagen), West Germany (Schlosspark-Theater, Berlin) and Belgium (Fakkelteater, Antwerp).

1983 *Fen* staged by Joint Stock and transferred later that year to Joseph Papp's Public Th., New York. Won OBIE for *Top Girls*. *Top Girls* premiered in Australia (Nimrod Th., Sydney), Sweden (Dramaten, Stockholm), Japan (Bungei-za Le Pilier, Tokyo), West Germany (Schauspielhaus, Cologne), Greece (National Th., Athens) and

Switzerland (Schauspielhaus, Zurich). *Vinegar Tom* premiered in New Zealand (Th. Corporate, Auckland). *Cloud Nine* premiered in Brazil (Rio de Janeiro).

1984 *Softcops* revised, and staged by RSC at the Barbican Pit. Wrote dialogue for *Midday Sun,* staged at the ICA. Won Susan Smith Blackburn Award (for best new play by an American or British woman dramatist) for *Fen. Top Girls* premiered in Denmark (Aarhus Theater), Norway (Rogaland Theater, Stavanger), New Zealand (Th. Corporate, Auckland) and Yugoslavia (Modern Th., Belgrade).

1985 *Owners* premiere in Switzerland (Schauspielhaus, Zurich). *Cloud Nine* premiered in Norway (Homansbyen Teaterselskap, Oslo). *Top Girls* premiered in Finland (Vaasa City Th.) and Holland (Schouwburg Het Park Te Horn, Amsterdam). *Fen* premiered in New Zealand (Th. Corporate, Auckland), West Germany (Schauspielhaus, Dusseldorf) and Norway (Vikateatret, Oslo).

1986 Wrote *A Mouthful of Birds* jointly with David Lan after workshop with Joint Stock, who staged it. Wrote *Serious Money. Cloud Nine* premiered in Austria (Volkstheater, Vienna), *Top Girls* premiered in Iceland (Alpyduleikhusid, Reykjavik) and Austria (Ensemble Th., Vienna).

1987 *Serious Money* staged at Royal Court, transferred to Wyndham's, and later to Joseph Papp's Public Th., New York. Awards for *Serious Money*: *Time Out*, Playwriting; *City Limits*, Best Play; *Evening Standard*, Best Comedy; *Plays and Players*, Best Play; Laurence Olivier Awards, Best Play and the Susan Smith Blackburn Award. Peruvian premiere of *Top Girls* (Quinta Rueda, Lima). *A Mouthful of Birds* premiered in Australia (Wharf Studio, Sydney) and West Germany (Bremen).

1988 American premiere of *Serious Money* at the Royale Th., New York, her first play on Broadway. With choreographer Ian Spink, writes *Fugue*, transmitted June.

The Plays

These plays up to and including *Angel* on p. 13, all written between 1961 and 1972, remain unperformed, and are not available for performance.

The Finnsburg Fragment

Play in three acts.

The lengthy story of Finn, Hildeburh and Hengest, from the 50-line Anglo-Saxon epic poem, The Finnsburg Fragment, *and from* Beowulf.

The Swimming Club

Television play.

A fascist group, led by Carl, comes to power and is opposed by Merrick and Frieda. Merrick's belief in freedom of speech hampers his attempts to defeat Carl, and he ends in prison.

Lee

Play in one act.

Sara Edwards is dead. Vin, her lover, accuses her father of killing her by destroying their relationship because Vin is black. Lee, the son of Edwards's employer, and Vin harass Edwards and his other daughter, Jane.

The Marriage of Toby's Idea of Angela and Toby's Idea of Angela's Idea of Toby

Play in nine scenes.

Scenes from the marriage of Toby and Angela, and their expectations of each other. The many other characters are played by puppets, dummies and two masked actors.

The Loonies

Television play.

Rose and Eric, once patients in a psychiatric hospital, live together. She leaves him and lives with George, who admits he finds her madness exciting. Rose and Eric return to the hospital together.

The Hospital at the Time of the Revolution

Play in ten scenes.

Fanon, in his Algerian psychiatric hospital, sees French torturers and their victims. He supports the Algerian revolution. Partly based on Chapter 5 of Fanon's The Wretched of the Earth.

Comic Strips from the Chinese

Play in fifteen scenes.

Power struggles within the state of Ch'i, about 600 BC, are

11

contrasted with the philosophy of Lieh-tzu, and interspersed with stories taken from his teachings.

Angel

Television play.

An angel accompanies the characters and at the end is welcomed. Prefaced by a quotation from Rilke, later used in the first published version of Fen.

Downstairs

Play in one act.
First production: Oriel College Dramatic Society, Oxford, 4 Nov. 1958 (dir. Wilfred De'Ath) and at the NUS/*Sunday Times* Student Drama Festival, London University, 1 Jan. 1959.

Susan feels that her family is being taken from her by its involvement with the family downstairs. She tells her son, Ted, to end his relationship with Catherine from downstairs. Ted kills Catherine. Susan knows they will never be free of her.

You've No Need to be Frightened

Radio play, written 1959, when a tape was made by Patrick Garland.

John longs to be free to climb the mountain. His wife tries to stop him. Finally she lets him go.

Having a Wonderful Time

Play in eight scenes.

First production: amateur student group, Questors Theatre, Ealing, 1960 (dir. E. Gilbert).

Paul, as narrator, tells the story of his holiday romances in the south of France. Partly in verse.

Easy Death

Play in three acts.
First Production: Oxford University Experimental Theatre Club, Oxford Playhouse, 9-10 Mar. 1962 (dir. Paul Burge).

Jack has made a fortune but isn't happy. Steve has come to his town and believes happiness is not to be found. Steve accidentally shoots Jack. Partly in verse.

Two plots at different times at different speeds, uniting in the third act, attempt to combine satire and straight writing by stylized action, songs and verse.

Churchill, programme note to first production

The Ants

Twenty-five-minute radio play.
Transmitted: BBC Third Programme, 27 Nov. 1962
(dir. Michael Bakewell; with David Palmer as Tim and Lockwood West as Grandfather).
Published: in *New English Dramatists, 12: Radio Plays,*
ed. Irving Wardle (Harmondsworth: Penguin, 1968), p. 91-103.

Beneath the not-quite-focused surface I found it a very beautiful, achieved small play: a small boy is sitting on a terrace playing with his friends the ants. Somewhere a war is going on. One of our bombs has killed ten thousand of 'them'. His mother and father come. Each tries to persuade the child to live with him. The child is baffled. They go. The old grandfather tells the child we are all alone; we all destroy each other. Together the boy and the war destroy the ants. This is all. Its beauty and its distinction lay for me in the fact that the note was not the note of misanthropy.

Martin Shuttleworth, *The Listener*, 6 Dec. 1962

Its strength as a radio piece is that it immediately hits the imagination with a bold metaphor from which the remainder of the action develops. . . . The traditional alliance between youth and age provides a double perspective on the scurrying life in between; and the bleak conclusion on human withdrawal is so forcefully projected by the image that Caryl Churchill has no need to put it into words.

Irving Wardle, Introduction,
New English Dramatists, 12, p. 19

I thought of it as a television play. I hadn't realized, I think, what a visual medium radio is at that point.

Churchill, interviewed by Geraldine Cousin in
'The Common Imagination and the Individual Voice',
New Theatre Quarterly, IV, 13 (Feb. 1988), p. 3

Lovesick

Thirty-minute radio play.
Transmitted: BBC Third Programme, 8 Apr. 1967 (dir. John Tydeman; with Anthony Hall as Hodge and Gudrun Ure as Ellen).

Dr Hodge, a psychiatrist, tells the case history of Ellen, and his attempts, using aversion therapy, to change people's sexual preferences. Max, Ellen's former lover, changes clothes and roles with his wife.

John Tydeman makes me feel that the whole thing is just so easy. The magic wand is waved, and it's coming out of the medium just the way it sounded in your head.

Churchill, interviewed by John F. O'Malley
in 'Caryl Churchill, David Mercer, and Tom Stoppard:
a Study of Contemporary British Dramatists Who Have Written for

Radio,Television and Stage'. Unpublished dissertation,
Florida State University, 1974, p. 30

Identical Twins

Thirty-five-minute radio play.
Transmitted: BBC Radio 3, 21 Nov. 1968
(dir. John Tydeman; with Kenneth Haigh as Teddy and Clive).

*The twins deliver monologues, sometimes simultaneously.
People have always confused one for the other. Clive kills
himself and Teddy takes over his lover, children and farm.*

She didn't know how difficult technically it was to do. It is a fact that we
had to record twin A and then sync [synchronize] twin B, who was
played by the same actor. He had to wear head caps to keep in sync with
himself because the two twins had different personalities. You could not
use the same tape and double it up because one is more forceful than the
other, so although they are saying the same thing at times, they have to
say it in a slightly similar way but in two different voices. Now it is a
physical fact that you can't do that for more than about thirty seconds,
keeping in sync with yourself. Blows the mind. Kenneth Haigh sat down
and said this is going to be easy but sort of cracked up around the third
sentence.

John Tydeman, interviewed by John F. O'Malley,
as above, p. 35

Abortive

Twenty-minute radio play.
Transmitted: BBC Radio 3, 4 Feb. 1971 (dir. John Tydeman;
with Prunella Scales as Roz and Dinsdale Landen as Colin).

*Roz and Colin, in bed, talk about the effects on them both of
Roz's abortion, and of their ambivalent attitudes to the rapist,
Billy.*

15

[Billy is] a third party who sort of lurks in a catalytic kind of way. . . .
Billy was and still continues to be a strange necessity in their lives.
>> John Tydeman, interviewed by John F. O'Malley,
>> as above, p. 36

Not ... Not ... Not ... Not ... Not Enough Oxygen

Twenty-five-minute radio play.
Transmitted: BBC Radio 3, 31 Mar. 1971 (dir. John Tydeman; with
John Hollis as Mick).

*In 2010, Mick and Vivian live in a tower block in a world short
of air, food and freedom. Claude, Mick's successful son, has
become a 'fanatic', and plans suicide.*

Caryl Churchill is a writer with an obvious talent for the medium. This
time she gave us a depressing but all too possible picture of city life in
the not very distant future, with three people gasping for air in a tower
block. A grave new world, convincingly caught.
>> Eva Figes, *The Listener*, 15 July 1971

Sort of to do with the Vietnam protests at the time.
>> Churchill, interviewed by Catherine Itzin, in *Stages in the Revolution*
>> (London: Methuen, 1980), p. 281

Schreber's Nervous Illness

Fifty-minute radio play, based on *Memoirs of my Nervous Illness*
by Daniel Paul Schreber, a nineteenth-century judge who became
schizophrenic.
Transmitted: BBC Radio 3, 25 July 1972 (dir. John Tydeman; with
Kenneth Haigh as Schreber).
First London production: King's Head Th., 5 Dec. 1972
(with Kenneth Haigh as Schreber).

[It] consists of a series of medical reports read by Kenneth Haigh. The reports are on the mental state of Herr Schreber, a former President of the Dresden Court of Appeal, while he was a patient in an asylum, and Mr. Haigh gives a coldly factual reading of them and also of Schreber's own contradictions.

As an insight into the imaginative excesses of a mind gone mad, the text is informative, but it gains nothing from such an undramatic presentation, for Mr. Haigh's objective approach limits his commitment to the subject.

Schreber's mental progress towards supposed female characteristics has a curious logic about it, but the chief object of his wild imaginings is his relationship to God, a morbid egoism which places Him at Schreber's own nerve ends. The material is promising, but in practice it is by no means as challenging as one feels it ought to have been.

DFB, 'Lunchtime: Images in Mind',
The Stage and Television Today, 14 Dec. 1972, p. 22

It worked much better on the radio.

Churchill, interviewed by John F. O'Malley,
as above, p. 42

The Judge's Wife

Thirty-minute television play.
Transmitted: BBC 2, 2 Oct. 1972 (dir. James Ferman; with
Rachel Kempson as Caroline and Sebastian Shaw as Laurence).

Was the Judge really the Fascist pig everyone believed him to be or was he, as his widow passionately avowed, a revolutionary manqué, an apparent pillar of the Establishment whose pose as the parody of a right wing bigot was a deliberate subterfuge to encourage revolt against the very things he seemed to stand for?

That was the intriguing question posed by Caryl Churchill on Monday in a play of considerable intellectual content but one in which it was difficult to believe. Not because the premise itself was so outrageous — indeed it opened fascinating vistas and

17

offered a possible rationale for the behaviour of certain politicians — but because of the occasional anomalies in story line and dialogue. . . .

The Judge's Wife was in short one of those plays which leave the critic with a strong sense of frustration, seeing so much originality just failing in the event to fulfil its promise.

Patrick Campbell, *The Stage and Television Today*, 5 Oct. 1972, p. 12

I don't know whether it's the way I feel about television or whether that play is something slightly . . . well, slick is the wrong word, but it's toward slick. It was a slightly deliberate case of seeing whether I could write a television play.

Churchill, interviewed by John F. O'Malley, as above, p. 49

Henry's Past

One-hour radio play.
Transmitted: BBC Radio 3, 5 Dec. 1972 (dir. John Tydeman; with Michael Bryant as Henry and Sheila Allen as Alice).

Henry has in the past attacked and maimed Geoffrey, who now is confined to a wheelchair and is married to Henry's former wife, Alice. The action concerns the visit of Alice and her family to Henry.

I wanted to get across the feeling of [Henry] accepting [life] as difficult and . . . involving actual people, whereas before it had all been something past, which he could no longer fit in at all, and had to keep . . . arranging into some kind of neat thing he could come to terms with. . . . I was feeling fairly sure that I knew what I was doing when I wrote short, and I wanted to see what happened when I wrote long. . . . A lot . . . of unnecessary extra introspection went into it.

Churchill, interviewed by John F. O'Malley, as above, p. 50

Owners

Play in two acts.

First London production: Royal Court Th. Upstairs, 6 Dec. 1972
(dir. Nicholas Wright; des. Di Seymour; with Stephanie Bidmead as
Marion, who took over the part after previews from Jill Bennett, who
was injured).
First New York production: Mercer-Shaw Th., 14 May 1973
(dir. Terese Hayden; des. Fred Kolouch; with Jacqueline Brookes as
Marion).
Revived: Young Vic Th., 6 Apr. 1987 (dir. Annie Castledine;
des. Mark Thompson; with Lucinda Curtis as Marion).
Published: London: Methuen, 1973; and in *Plays: One.*

*Marion is a domineering property-developer, married to Clegg,
a Crippenesque butcher. She buys and sells a house in which the
top flat is occupied by her former lover Alec and his family. She
tries to drive them out of the flat, ostensibly to boost the value of
the property, but really to demonstrate her power over them.
Her methods succeed, but not quite in the way she expects. Alec
refuses to leave, his wife Lisa is pregnant and she becomes
hysterical beneath the subtle bullying. In the midst of this
hysteria she offers her unborn child for adoption by Marion and
Clegg. The child is born — and handed over: as soon as the
papers have been signed, Lisa regrets the adoption. Her
unhappiness, which is deeply felt by Alec, makes Marion all the
more determined to hang on to the child. If Marion can't have
Alec, she'll ruin his marriage. Eventually, Alec and Lisa get
their child back, but Marion in revenge orders her hatchetman,
Worsley, to burn down their house. Alec dies in the blaze. . . .*

Beneath the plotting and the jokes Miss Churchill seems to be asking
several important questions. What does 'ownership' mean? Does the
landlord own his flat — or does the tenant? Is the physical mother the
real parent to a child — or the legal foster-mother? To what extent can a
human being either possess his own life or control the lives of others?
Even Alec . . . terminates the life of his senile mother and regains his
freedom and will-power by doing so. The argument is therefore
complicated, despite the black-and-white characterizations. But the play
fails for want of the most elementary dramatic disciplines: namely unity
of action and unity of tone — those much despised classical standards.

John Elsom, *The Listener*, 21 Dec. 1972, p. 874

The parable about property owning is . . . no more than the foundation
upon which the far more complex statement of the rest of the play rests;

19

for the question which it poses through the characters of Worsley, the unsuccessful suicide, and Alec, the man who has lost all desire to participate in life, is a question on a far higher plane. If all our activity, all our hustle and bustle, centres around some form of possession — money, houses or possessing children, lovers and wives — what is there beyond it, once we have recognized the futility of possessions? The figure of Alec's mother, who is so old that she has become little more than a vegetable . . . indicates the basic emptiness of our existence. The play therefore seems to me to pose the need for a content in our lives which might transcend the search for material fulfilment, in other words the need for some sort of metaphysical dimension. Alec dies in the fire, laid by Worsley on Clegg's bidding, while trying to rescue another family's baby. Does that point towards a philosophy of love through self-sacrifice, a higher order of love than the striving for mere possession of the other person?

It is not at all essential to know the answer to that question. It is sufficient that the play poses it and starts one on such trains of thinking.

Martin Esslin, *Plays and Players*, Feb. 1973, p. 41-2

Miss Churchill's weakness is that she throws everything in bar the kitchen sink: euthanasia, body-snatching, the Protestant work ethic, the use of sex for social revenge. She also manipulates character to prove her social points: you don't really believe in the property tycoon's physical lust for her tenant, in her bookish butcher-husband who is a caricature of male chauvinist piggery or in the suicidal tendencies of her industrious legman. However Miss Churchill writes with real knowledge of the harassment used by landlords to evict perfectly blameless tenants and argues with assurance her key point that the law is based on property rather than on morals.

Nicholas Wright's production rightly opts for fragmented nervy realism and Stephanie Bidmead admirably brings out the heroine's blend of vulgarity and vulnerability.

Michael Billington, *The Guardian*, 13 Dec. 1972

Nicholas Wright's production, spread out over the floor of the little theatre, is swift and ingenious, and the performances are uniformly admirable. I felt only that there were moments when the play sprawled unnecessarily. Miss Churchill writes, as most of today's writers do, in a mosaic of short scenes, rather than longer ones where development can be seen taking place. One or two of them struck me as rather cumbersome machinery to establish single facts that could as well be brought, more economically, into the dialogue of more essential passages. However her characterization is so acute, and her dialogue so amusing, that it is perhaps churlish of me to wish for any less of them.

B. A. Young, *Financial Times*, 13 Dec. 1972

Miss Churchill possesses creative gifts that are almost singular among her contemporaries: a poetic imagination, an idiosyncratic vision of reality, and a sense of variousness in her characters, even when she clearly dislikes them.

Owners has its longueurs, and its several plot strands are insufficiently integrated, but it brings a genuine human voice into a theatre which has lately been suffering not a little from stridency and polemicism. This is not to say that her play lacks social or political meaning — actually, it is charged with such meaning — but rather that her themes are subtly evoked through the interplay of character and action. . . .

I am among those who will watch Miss Churchill's future progress with a keen sense of anticipation.

Robert Brustein, 'Subjects of Scandal and Concern',
The Observer, 17 Dec. 1972

Into it went for the first time a lot of things that had been building up in me over a long time, political attitudes as well as personal ones.

Churchill, interviewed by Catherine Itzin,
in *Stages in the Revolution*, p. 282

There were two ideas really. This happens quite a lot. I've got several ideas and then I suddenly see a way, while I'm working on one, that the others can be put into the same play. There was one idea going about landlords and tenants, and then another about western aggressiveness and eastern passivity, and I realized that obviously the two could go together. . . . At that point the landlord became a woman, because that made the distinction better than if I'd had an active man and a passive woman. So all that slotted together.

One of the difficulties with it [is] that it comes in and out of being more or less real. In the same way it comes in and out of being funny. One of the things that happens in the play is the juxtaposing of things that one accepts the existence of perfectly well if they're in their own context, but taken out of context, set up against each other, they make each other absurd or unpleasant. And this in itself throws up a style which isn't naturalistic. That's why the playing has to be kept sharp, or parts of the play could seem like clichéd naturalistic scenes, whereas things which might be naturalistic should really be thrown up at funny angles. . . . I'm very often conscious of the absurd things people take for granted, and the whole different systems people have for judging whether things are important or not.

Churchill, interviewed by Steve Gooch,
in 'Caryl Churchill', *Plays and Players*, Jan. 1973, p. 40-1

Owners got so many scenes in it not in fact because it was really more like a television or radio play, but because, in a funny way, I was trying to make it more like a stage play, because to me in my mind at that point, a radio play was where I could interminably go on with people talking about what went on in their heads. . . . I desperately wanted to see if I could make things happen. . . . Next time I don't think I'd need to have so many scenes because now I've got the confidence to realize that I can make things happen.

Churchill, interviewed by John F. O'Malley,
as above, p.50

We accept as part of the pattern of everyday life the fact that old houses are bought up by certain people and developed. We put their activity in the context of a regular system of events. When I attempt to look at property development in the play from a slightly shifted angle . . . then I hope we can see this sort of activity more clearly for what it is — it becomes more a question of whether you think of people . . . [being] as important as yourself, with feelings, or as objects to be dealt with. . . . The owners of the title are concerned with various types of ownership. There's ownership of property and things, extended into the idea of owning and controlling people. Really it goes back to the whole idea of Western individualism, and capitalism and progress, as opposed to the more passive Eastern idea of simply being. I'm concerned with the whole idea of individualism that developed with Christianity, and the puritan idea of work as a virtue, and aggressive achievement, and having a definite idea of one's character and purpose in life. This is another regular context or system that we accept and act within. Against this background I include a character who is completely passive. He's there really because of an interest I had in the Taoist Chinese idea of being: of not actually doing or achieving anything, but just being. I'm not proposing this as a marvellous answer, but by putting it alongside the other system, I hope that each will question the other.

Churchill, interviewed by John Hall, in 'Close Up',
The Guardian, 12 Dec. 1972

Owners is a bleak vision of a society whose values are reduced to the level of poverty and wealth creation, of a group of powerless people in the hands of a dominant woman, and of absurd men plotting their own and others' downfall. It has become starkly relevant, whereas once it was a more philosophical debate on the nature of individual power-sharing. Though by no means an overtly political play, it would seem more than ever capable of being interpreted on a wider level.

John Vidal, *The Guardian*, 9 Apr. 1987

Perfect Happiness

Thirty-minute radio play.
Transmitted: BBC Radio 3, 30 Sept. 1973 (dir. John Tydeman;
    with Jill Bennett as Felicity).
First London production: Soho Poly, lunch-time, 10 Mar. 1975
    (dir. Susanna Capon; des. Sarah Paulley; with Eleanor Bron as
    Felicity).

A distressed wife invites two of her husband's girl friends home after his unexplained absence for a night. In the kitchen, while making and actually baking a cake, her questions become gradually more frantic as she probes into their relationship with her husband. . . .

J.B., *Daily Telegraph,* 11 Mar. 1975

Caryl Churchill's transplanted radio sketch is a woefully anaemic and inconclusive foray into Woman's Lib territory that fumbles inconsequentially with 'the role of a woman in a male-dominated society' but fails to deal with any issue in a fundamental, let alone theatrical, manner. Words and phrase-making, gestures and mystery. Miss Churchill sells herself short by allowing this sort of thing on stage.

Michael Coveney, *Financial Times*, 11 Mar. 1975

Directed by Susanna Capon, the production is set in a realistic and, I imagine, expensive kitchen designed by Sarah Paulley. But the behaviour exhibited by Eleanor Bron as the wife and Catherine Kessler as one of the secretaries adds nothing realistic to the text; and while

Jennie Stoller as the other secretary exhibits an aggression that might add a dimension to the script if the whole production cut loose from its realistic trappings, she is making her statement in a vacuum. . . .

This is the kind of lunchtime theatre that will replace neither lunchtime nor theatre.

Charles Lewson, *The Times*, 18 Mar. 1975

Turkish Delight

Thirty-five-minute television play.
Transmitted: BBC 2, 22 Apr. 1974 (dir. Herbert Wise; with Julia Foster as the Call Girl).

A prostitute comes to a party dressed as an Eastern dancing girl in order to reveal a famous client's sexual fantasies. His ex-wife and fiancée dress the same. They discover he has involved them all in the same fantasy and leave. Episodes of plot alternate with monologues from each woman.

Objections to Sex and Violence

Play in two acts.
First London production: Royal Court Th., 2 Jan. 1975
     (dir. John Tydeman; des. David Short; with Rosemary McHale as Jule and Anna Calder-Marshall as Annie).
Published: in *Plays by Women*, Vol. 4, ed. Michelene Wandor
     (London: Methuen, 1985).

[It concerns] a middle-class woman coming to political consciousness and trying to break away from her class roots. The heroine has been seduced by anarchists, and is somehow involved with and committed to indiscriminate civilian bombings, though the cause is never specified. Her friends and family attempt to woo her back to non-violence, without success.

Catherine Itzin, *Stages in the Revolution*, p. 282

Caryl Churchill's new play feels more like a chamber work for voices than a fully realized dramatic event in a medium-sized theatre. Several commentators have noted an uneasiness about the setting up of the duologues which are the play's mode, a lack of conviction in the sheer mechanics of pushing a pair of speakers on and off. . . .

Ms. Churchill does nothing so crude as to write in parallel lines. The connections are there to be picked up or not. She avoids clearly pinning her characters down with issues. She has a way of sidling up to her themes and giving them a nudge which is both fascinating and maddening. . . .

There are many telling moments in the dialogue. . . . Ms. Churchill is excellent on the instability of words like 'hurt' and 'belief', the absurdity of concepts like 'happiness' and 'non-violence'. But of course these things make for a largely static and wordy piece of theatre. . . . It reminds me at times of Edward Bond, by which I mean the highest praise. The sheer economy and resonance of Bond's stagecraft is unsurpassed amongst contemporary dramatists. Ms. Churchill may be going to alter that assessment. At any rate, she's going to be a major dramatist.

W. Stephen Gilbert, *Plays and Players*,
Mar. 1975, p. 24-5

It is all there: liberalism, the National Front, hard-line Socialism, and the terrorist ethic (if that is the right word). But theatrically speaking who cares? I suspect that even Miss Churchill does not care very much, as what gets spoken about on stage differs totally from what happens. So far as events and immediate feelings are concerned we are back in the traditional feminine world where personal relationships are all and everything would work out satisfactorily if men would only behave properly.

With the possible exception of Terry, the Communist husband, each of the men makes his exit with a knife from the author quivering between the shoulder blades. . . .

John Tydeman's production fails equally to animate the characters as generalized social types, or to endow them with any individual life that one can care about. . . . This is a difficult time for playwrights; but I doubt whether anything is to be gained from going through the motions of writing about important issues when one has nothing to say.

Irving Wardle, 'An Unfilled Portmanteau', *The Times*, 3 Jan. 1975

Objections to Sex and Violence [is] . . . something of a morality play without a moral. Its characters, that is to say, are all firmly representative of some class or attitude of mind, rather too much so for the good of the play, yet deployed with a short-term intelligence which makes them interesting moment-by-moment without leaving behind any clear impression of what Miss Churchill is saying, or indirectly expressing by their interplay. . . . Miss Churchill's conclusion would seem to be that the connection between sex and violence is that both can be satisfactorily exercised at someone else's expense, but that people who don't so exercise them are all failures.

J. W. Lambert, *Drama*, Spring 1975, p. 43-5

I found the first act in particular often tediously talkative, and . . . there are irrelevancies, such as the death of Terry's father, that seemed to me to add nothing to the design, but prolonged the play beyond its capacity to hold the attention. Plots are not just old-fashioned tricks to split the ears of the groundlings; they are valuable machinery intended to clarify themes. The fact that Miss Churchill's theme is indecision doesn't excuse her.

B. A. Young, *Financial Times*, 4 Jan. 1975

The play is a conversation piece with annoying vestiges of plot. I tried approaching it as a Shavian fantasia, but kept stubbing my toes on doggedly naturalistic fragments of character and dialogue, fragments which refused to build into any kind of structure. . . .

Even verbally the play never really coheres. The characters' sexual and political attitudes are mechanically aligned, rather than dramatically knotted. Each scene divides in half: first, let's talk about sex, then about violence. Intellectually we can see where the issues join, but then we always could.

Robert Cushman, 'On the Beach', *The Observer*, 5 Jan. 1975

Moving Clocks Go Slow

Play in two acts.
First London production: Royal Court Th. Upstairs, Sunday-night production, 15 June 1975 (dir. John Ford; with Aviva Goldkorn as Kay and Nicholas Ball as Rocket).

Caryl Churchill's 'space-play' is a Miltonic allegory in terms of science fiction. The world is ruled by a revered figure in a space

*suit, Agent Fox; the great desire of its people is to go 'outward',
that is, to the half-mythical realm of outer space. Agent Fox's
adversary is a black-clad spy, Q. He and Fox are on familiar
terms, though Q is the reporting centre for all the disloyal and
dishonest of the earth. At the focus of the terrestials whose fate
we follow is Kay . . . a woman operator in an 'outward'
immigration office who is brought back to earth by two aliens
posing as a fellow-operator and a Psychokinetic Android
Labourer, built to look like a human girl. Kay is joined by her
mother, who has become a tramp . . .; her daughter . . . lately
released from a prison sentence for killing her children; and her
former boy-friend Rocket . . . , a flash boy with a private line
to Q.*

Having established this universe and hurled her characters into it,
Miss Churchill does little more than stir them about while invading
invisible aliens take over the earth and so provoke Agent Fox to destroy
it. Deeper study would, I am sure, detect a number of allegorical
parallels, but when her creatures' adventures are so unadventurous there
is hardly enough urge to uncover them.

B. A. Young, *Financial Times*, 16 June 1975

I felt that the director, John Ford, had been carried away by sheer words
— or should it be mere words? — and the force of Andy Hellaby's
sound effects, so that the force of what was meant was spread too thin.
One hour would have done, for me at any rate, quite nicely.

M.A.M., *The Stage*, 10 July 1975, p. 9

Save It for the Minister

Thirty-minute television play.
Written: with Mary O'Malley and Cherry Potter.
Transmitted: BBC 2, *Eleventh Hour*, 26 July 1975 (dir. Piers Haggard;
with Jane Asher as The Woman, Stefan Kalipha as The Man, and
Nadia Cattouse as The Minister).

*The Man (black) and The Woman (white) discuss their
grievances about racial and gender discrimination at work.
Their case is accepted by the Minister for Equal Rights. She,*

however, can do nothing about gender and racial oppression in general, imaged in the play in surrealistic scenes.

Light Shining in Buckinghamshire

Play in two acts.
Written: after workshop with Joint Stock Theatre Group.
First production: by Joint Stock Theatre Group; first performed
   at the Traverse Th., Edinburgh, 7 Sept. 1976 (dir. Max Stafford-Clark;
   des. Sue Plummer; music Colin Sell; with Janet Chappell (succeeded
   by Carole Hayman), Linda Goddard, Bob Hamilton, Will Knightley,
   Colin McCormack and Nigel Terry); first performed in London at the
   Royal Court Th. Upstairs, 27 Sept. 1976.
Revived: Tranter Th. Company; first performance 1 Oct. 1988,
   Buddle Arts Centre, Wallsend, and on tour (dir. Padraig Tolan; with
   Sue Hoyle and David Linton).
Published: London: Pluto Press, 1978; and in *Plays: One.*

For a short time when the king had been defeated [in the civil war in the seventeenth century] anything seemed possible, and the play shows the amazed excitement of people taking hold of their own lives, and their gradual betrayal as those who led them realized that freedom could not be had without property being destroyed. . . . The Levellers and Diggers were crushed by the Army, and many turned in desperation to the remaining belief in the millennium, that Christ would come to do what they had failed in. The last long scene of the play is a meeting of Ranters, whose ecstatic and anarchic belief in economic and sexual freedom was the last desperate burst of revolutionary feeling before the Restoration.

Churchill, Introduction to the play in Plays: One

One of the dramatic virtues of this magnificent play is that it can assume a certain given historical foundations and proceed to de-emphasize specific characters and events. In fact the play's history is rooted wholly in a *collective* consciousness which is its protagonist and hero. This is neither a group of specified individuals moving together or even a defined community experiencing the raising of armies or the aftermath of civil war, but an interweaving of historical and fictional persons appearing and disappearing, together and independently, through the middle of the seventeenth century, seeking parallel roads to freedom, paths occasionally crossing, reaching similar (if not cohesive) conclusions. Churchill works against their identification: 'there is no need for the audience to know each time which character they are seeing'. Consequently, roles are interchanged so that no one player carries the same character throughout, thereby stressing the collective vision of history even in the staging of the play. Initially this is confusing, but Churchill does not feel constrained by the pre-eminence of personality in our culture (and in our theatre), and twists our comprehension of inter-relationships in her view of events and in her operation of the stage. The brilliant collective playing of Joint Stock in Max Stafford-Clark's production first makes her style seem palatable, and finally correct and necessary. . . .

Those who have gathered at the final prayer meeting learn not to expect their freedom to be granted them . . . but that it must be taken, by them, and not in false solidarity with any other class. They are left with an ecstatic solidarity of their own — 'all things in common' — and a sense of power (both men and women) for common future use. . . .

Light Shining in Buckinghamshire [is] one of the finest pieces of English playwriting for years.

David Zane Mairowitz, 'God and the Devil ',
Plays and Players, Feb. 1977, p. 24

If I were to be asked to list the plays which have given me most satisfaction this year, this would come pretty high on the list. Two features of this production impressed me very much. First of all, there was the complexity of its concern: many important questions were raised and no trite answers offered. On the face of it an account of the English Revolution, this is in fact a genuine study of revolution itself, any revolution. When, towards the end, one of the actors suggests that a great opportunity has been lost, one is not given the feeling that a point is being made, but that a question has been seriously asked. Moreover, an even more important question is asked by the religious beliefs and expectations of the characters — is there a direct correlation between the efficiency of a revolution and the nature of the society that creates it? In other words, what kind of omelette do you get when you break rotten eggs? Parallels with our own time exist in plenty — the scene depicting the Putney debates reminded me very much of the squabbles of the British Labour Party — but they operate at several levels and do not exist merely as parallels. The second feature which impresses is the language: spare, uncluttered, colourful when it needs to be, usually low-keyed and neutral, the awareness of the importance of the language is always evident. Whether this is a feature of the play or the company — I have noticed the same quality in Joint Stock's previous productions — I could not say, but it is a delight to listen to nevertheless.

Donald Campbell, 'Traditional Movement',
Plays and Players, Nov. 1976, p. 20-1

I found some of the sermonizing dialogue heavy going. The hectoring self-confidence of the exploiters, and the pathetic gullibility of their victims, makes for truthful reportage but slow-moving drama.

John Barber, *Daily Telegraph*, 28 Sept. 1976

Numerous points of contact with the modern world, such as the treatment of vagrants and squatters, crop up naturally; but only in one scene, where a butcher stands, cleaver in hand, bellowing his refusal to serve a meat-gorged customer, is the connection ever underlined. There are no personal heroes or villains.

Cromwell, on the one occasion he appears, is presented as an affable negotiator. Nor is there any attempt to minimize the remoteness of seventeenth-century mental landscape. The production takes place against a skull and hourglass and resounds with the contorted intensities of millenarian rhetoric which Miss Churchill has succeeded in dovetailing with her own dialogue.

In its present form, the piece is burdened by a prolonged final scene and six separate epilogues. Otherwise it is a model of expressive brevity, each scene, no matter how powerfully charged, cut off as if by a guillotine as the actor steps out of character. . . .

Handling the spare properties as if they were sacramental objects, walled within inward-turning smiles and harsh, statuesque attitudes, their very features seem to belong to another century: which redoubles its contact with ours.

Irving Wardle, *The Times*, 28 Sept. 1976

A colleague pejoratively described the play as 'committed' but I would have said its chief commitment was to truth since it unflinchingly shows the intolerance that was the obverse side of the demand for common justice. Deftly, it sketches in the kind of social conditions . . . that led to hunger for revolution. But it also shows that the primitive Christianity that fostered such revolution contained its own cruelties. . . .

Clearly the burden of the piece is that revolutionary idealism was betrayed by Parliament and the Army. But its great virtue is that it sets the evidence before us and makes no attempt to load the dice through presentational effects. . . .

Beautifully directed by Max Stafford-Clark and finely acted by the whole company . . . the play has an austere eloquence that precisely matches its subject.

Michael Billington, *The Guardian*, 28 Sept. 1976

We had debates in the workshops and talks about specific historical characters. We read a lot and talked about moments of amazing change and extraordinariness in our own lives, things turned upside down. We got ourselves fluent with the Bible, so the whole area was opened up and everyone knew what it was about. . . .

A revolutionary belief in the millennium went through the Middle Ages and broke out strongly in England at the time of the civil war. Soldiers fought the king in the belief that Christ would come and establish heaven on earth. What was established instead was an authoritarian parliament, the massacre of the Irish, the development of capitalism.

Churchill, interviewed by Catherine Itzin,
in *Stages in the Revolution*, p. 283-4

With *Light Shining* I'd come with a very unfinished script, because I'd written a version which didn't work at all. So then I wrote another version in the ten days before rehearsals began, but it wasn't finished. There were half a dozen people being traced through the events, and everyone was going to perform minor parts in others' stories. But then we [Churchill and Max Stafford-Clark] had the idea jointly — we suggested it jokingly, and then came back to it: 'What we ought to do is let everybody play different parts, and not worry about characters going through.' That reduced the number of scenes it needed, and it made everybody's experience seem shared. In a war or a revolution the same things happen to a lot of people.

Churchill, interviewed by Ronald Hayman, in 'Double Acts',
Sunday Times Magazine, 2 Mar. 1980, p. 27

One scene involving a preacher and an objector at a prayer meeting caused particular trouble. . . . Producing a pack of tarot cards, . . . [Stafford-Clark] gave one card to each participant saying that the number on the card would govern whether we were to support the preacher or oppose him. Eight, nine or ten demanded vociferous support.

An entirely different subject was given to the preacher for his harangue — Welsh Nationalism instead of the theology of God's elected saints. No-one knew who had the joker, the objector's card. . . .

The meeting began with Colin McCormack speaking eloquently on the rights of Cymru. The objector, Jan Chappell, found so many hostile to her cries of outrage that she was forcibly thrown out of the room. We then discovered that Stafford-Clark had stacked the deck and dealt out three tens. The scene was conducted again, rewritten, and no longer presented problems of motivation.

Ann McFerran, 'Fringe Beneficiaries', *Time Out*,
24-30 Sept. 1976, p. 11

Vinegar Tom

Play in twenty-one scenes and seven songs.
Written: after discussion with Monstrous Regiment.
First production: by Monstrous Regiment, first performed at the
    Humberside Th., Hull, 12 Oct. 1976; first performed in London at the
    ICA Th., 14 Dec. 1976; trans. Half Moon Th., 17 Jan. 1977
    (dir. Pam Brighton; des. Andrea Montag; music Helen Glavin; with
    Roger Allam, Ian Blower, Chris Bowler, Linda Broughton,
    Josefina Cupido, Helen Glavin, Gillian Hanna, Mary McCusker, and
    Sue Todd).
Published: London: TQ Publications, 1978; in *Plays by Women:*
    Volume One, ed. Michelene Wandor (London: Methuen, 1982), and in
    Plays: One.

The central action of the play involves the scapegoating of poor women by . . . Jack and his wife Margery, a couple who are at high risk because of their attempts at economic expansion. . . . Margery cannot bear the pressure of feeling incompetent and undeserving; Jack needs a target for his sexual and financial frustration. Not wanting to believe that God judges them 'bad', they begin to interpret their misfortunes as acts of witchcraft committed by their poor neighbours, Joan and her daughter Alice. The Church provides the institutional mechanism for burning such witches; traditional prime targets are single women, economically marginal and sexually deviant from the puritan code. The accused include Ellen, the cunning woman or healer who earns her own living outside of the monetary system and works outside the sanctioned medical/male establishment; Alice, object of Jack's sexual desire, whom he accuses of making him impotent; and Susan, who has had an abortion for which she feels guilty. Internalizing the prevailing social and sexual code, Susan feels that she must have been a witch without knowing it. In her conflation of economic and moral codes, Susan shows how women can remain unconscious of their oppression and can victimize themselves and others. The only escapee from punishments of torture and death is Betty, the land owner's daughter. However, while she escapes class oppression, she pays the price of sexual submission: she agrees to marry and become the thing she dreads, 'a good wife'.

> Janelle Reinelt, 'Beyond Brecht: Britain's New Feminist Drama', *Theatre Journal*, XXXVIII, 2 (May 1986), p. 161

The impact [of the songs] is one of estrangement, especially when the lyrics become medically and physically graphic. . . . But the playtext is not strong enough to withstand the breaking of its rhythm and antagonism of the musical interludes. . . . Pam Brighton's production . . . (which clearly has the author's consent) does not override the conflict of its dramatic and musical pitches.

> David Zane Mairowitz, 'God and the Devil', *Plays and Players*, Feb. 1977, p. 24

Caryl Churchill's *Vinegar Tom* . . . may be set in the world of seventeenth-century witchcraft, but it speaks, through its striking images and its plethora of ironic contradictions, of and to this century's still deep-rooted anti-feminism and women's oppression. . . .

At one point the cunning woman explains the art of sinking without drowning (yet another irony, of course). What the play did, implicitly, was show how sinking without drowning is the art of survival as a woman, whether in the seventeenth or twentieth century.

Monstrous Regiment, a co-operative company who came together out of dissatisfaction with the opportunities offered to women working in the theatre, performed this play beautifully.

> Catherine Itzin, 'Survival — by Sinking without Drowning', *Tribune*, Dec. 1976, p. 8-9

The play falters in its lack of faith in dramatic analogy, let alone the power of the story as it stands. The music . . . , admittedly entertaining in itself, spells out the fact that we all need to find something to burn: if not a witch, then perhaps a woman, a black or a Jew. Such sentiment, although arguably admirable, is hardly achieved in the play itself. Or rather, it is *potentially* achieved and then tossed away in righteous overstatement.

Michael Coveney, Financial Times, 15 Dec. 1976

There was a meeting in which we talked about the fact that we were all thinking about witches, and they told me some of the books they'd read. I went off and read those and other books that I found. Then we met again, and we were all interested in women who were marginal to society being made scapegoats and seen as witches, rather than in witchcraft practices that might have been happening. And that was it: there were those two meetings and then I wrote it. During rehearsals there were changes — for instance, they'd got an extra member of the company by this time, so I added the character of Betty because they needed another part, but not too big a part because it was for someone who was mainly a musician. And there was some discussion at that point of what character could it be.

Churchill, in unpublished interview
with Linda Fitzsimmons, 20 April 1988

The form of *Vinegar Tom* was extremely bizarre. You had a series of quite naturalistic scenes punctuated by very modern songs in modern dress. It all came to some kind of conclusion, and then at the end you had two music-hall characters coming out of the blue, developing it nowhere. If you took out the music you would have something akin to a traditional play. But we knew that we had to have the music to smash that regular and acceptable theatrical form. We didn't sit down and say deliberately that we need to smash that form, but that is what we did nonetheless; I think we unconsciously felt a need to do that. . . .

What we were saying about witchcraft was not necessarily true only of witchcraft, but of women's experience today. We had a very real feeling that we didn't want to allow the audience to get off the hook by regarding it as a period piece, a piece of very interesting history. Now a lot of people felt their intelligence was affronted by that. They said: 'I don't know why these people have to punctuate what they are saying by these modern songs. We're perfectly able to draw conclusions about the world today from historical parallels.' Actually, I don't believe that and, in any case, we can't run that risk. For every single intelligent man who can draw parallels, there are dozens who don't. It's not that they can't. It's that they won't. I believe that the simple telling of the historical story, say, is not enough. It's always a question of choices and some things are always left out. You have to choose between what you keep in and what you leave out. It's at that point of choice where women on the whole find that they get left out.

Gillian Hanna, 'Feminism and Theatre',
Theatre Papers, Second Series, No. 8 (1978), p. 9-10

Vinegar Tom is a play about witches, but none of the characters portrayed is a witch; it's a play which doesn't talk about hysteria, evil or demonic possession but about poverty, humiliation and prejudice, and the view which the women accused of witch craft had of themselves.

Churchill, interviewed by Maggie Rose in 'A Woman's Point of View',
Sipario, Nov.-Dec. 1987, p. 99

'Vinegar Tom' is the name of a cat-like beast depicted on a seventeenth-century engraving along with Matthew Hopkins, the famous . . . witch-finder. The head resembles a bull's (with horns), the body is elongated like a greyhound's and the tail is thin and extremely long.

Programme note to production at Questors Theatre, 1 Mar. 1987

Traps

Play in two acts.
First London production: Royal Court Th. Upstairs, 27 Jan. 1977
(dir. John Ashford; des. Terry Jacobs; with Nigel Terry as Jack,
Catherine Kessler as Syl, Anthony Milner as Albert,
Tim Piggott-Smith as Reg, Catherine Neilson as Christie, and
Hugh Fraser as Del).
Published: London: Pluto Press, 1978; and in *Plays: One.*

As the play begins, the characters look as though they are trapped by their domestic and social problems. Syl . . . has a baby who keeps her awake and away from a job; whereas Jack . . . is a left-wing activist who thinks that he is being watched by the police. Albert . . . believes that he has an extra-sensory relationship with his sister, Christie . . . who is in trouble. Sooner or later, Christie will come to the flat where Albert lives with Jack and Syl, seeking support in escaping from her husband, Reg . . . a middle-class, successful wage-slave. The last member of the gang is Del . . . suspicious, jealous and arbitrary.

Miss Churchill then takes apart the different elements in their external lives and assembles them again in a changed order. The baby has not been born, they are all living in the country, not in a town flat, Christie is not trying to escape from Reg but doing her best to love him, and locked doors open. In this new puzzle — and a jigsaw lies on the floor — the characters remain identifiably the same, although they have been offered a different range of choices. The traps, therefore, are not external social ones, but internal ones of temperament and childhood conditioning. How can they escape from these traps which are part of their natures?

Miss Churchill gives no answer exactly (nor can one be given), but she gives an illustration of what it feels like temporarily to be released. They take a bath, one after another, Reg last, slowest in overcoming inhibitions. It is like Christian baptism, a way of washing off inherited sins. Then they eat communal soup, and smile at each other.

John Elsom, *The Listener*, 3 Feb. 1977

Traps, with its maxim that everything is possible on the stage, is, Churchill says, influenced by Peter Handke's *Ride Over Lake Constance*.

Renate Klett, ' "Anything's Possible in the Theatre": Portrait of Author Caryl Churchill', *Theater Heute*, Jan. 1984, p. 21

A fascinating script, always several pages ahead of the audience, especially on critics' night, offers plenty of sinewy lines and joyous juxtapositions and Churchill's most confident and creative deployment of stagecraft to date. The result is that one regrets the feeling of exclusion from an enigma where one might have resented being subjected to arbitrary mystification. . . . John Ashford's production is exemplary though I doubt that one is much the wiser for it.

W. Stephen Gilbert, *'Dusa, Fish, Stas and Vi . . . and Traps'*,
Plays and Players, Mar. 1977, p. 32

Caryl Churchill, a writer I admire, has come up with a trick play called *Traps*. . . . She traps her audience into thinking black is black and then blandly informs them it is white. . . .

Nothing is explained: this is not a mystery story. It is a facile exercise in mystification, a pseudo-intellectual joke.

J. B., *Daily Telegraph*, 28 Jan. 1977

Nothing in the play explains what brought this particular group of people together, or whether their fractious commune amounts to an attempt to escape the trap, or whether it is itself a trap of another kind. . . .

My complaint is not so much that the play is mysterious but that its characters arouse so little interest.

Irving Wardle, *The Times*, 28 Jan. 1977

Miss Churchill can write crisp dialogue and the company, under John Ashford's direction, speak it crisply if with little sign of enthusiasm. But as soon as I found out the tricks the author was playing I lost interest in the denizens of her little world; they had plenty to say to each other, but nothing to me.

B. A. Young, *Financial Times*, 28 Jan. 1977

Floorshow

Cabaret.
Written: with Michelene Wandor, Bryony Lavery, and David Bradford.
First London production: Monstrous Regiment at Th. Royal,
    Stratford East, 18 Jan. 1978 (dir. David Bradford;
    music Helen Glavin, Josefina Cupido and Roger Allam; with
    Roger Allam, Chris Bowler, Josefina Cupido, Helen Glavin,
    Gillian Hanna, Mary McCusker, and Clive Russell).

The women in . . . [Monstrous Regiment] wanted to explore the notion of glamour in the performance process, to show that women can be as funny as men, and, as individuals, to experiment with adlib exchanges with the audience. . . . Floorshow *was about women and work. . . . It included songs, monologues, sketches, comic patter about women and work in Africa, the idea of 'pin money', working as a bus conductor, reversed domestic roles, and the performers wore variegated, brightly coloured costumes — reminiscent of the variety of clown costumes, and with a bouncy uniformity which didn't make obvious sexual distinctions between the male and female performers.*

Michelene Wandor,
Carry On, Understudies: Theatre and Sexual Politics
(London: Routledge and Kegan Paul, 1986), p. 71

37

Floorshow is an amusing cabaret . . . so it cannot be expected to put very seriously or logically its proselytizing Women's Lib theme that women are hard done to in all sorts of jobs, from the shop floor to the kitchen sink.

Its flamboyant colours and noisily brilliant beat music appealed to a young audience more for the originality of the Monstrous Regiment touring group — two men and five women — than for its argument. Clad in strong reds, greens and blues — one man had sequinned braces — this unusual company, partly pierrot, partly band, sang and played into half a dozen microphones with tumbling rhythms and electronic accessories. The girls appeared to be against both domesticity at home and unworthy jobs outside and held the view that men were not worth much. . . .

There were songs and sketches about running houses, trade union troubles and sex discrimination. . . . It was altogether a lively do.

Harold Atkins, *Daily Telegraph*, 19 Jan. 1978

The After Dinner Joke

One-hour television play.
Transmitted: BBC 1, 14 Feb. 1978 (dir. Colin Bucksey; with
Paula Wilcox as Miss Selby).

Miss Selby works for businessman Price's organized charity. She learns the politics of charity, and that only political means can bring about solutions.

After Dinner Joke . . . had Paula Wilcox as a sort of Alice in Charity Land. The electronic whizzery involved, colour separation overlay, gave it a particularly bright and paint-box look like a living strip cartoon or a Pollock's Toy Theatre. Paula had a series of paradoxical encounters with characters who took their chance of a glittering solo.

Nancy Banks-Smith, 'Me Tarzan', *The Guardian*, 15 Feb. 1978

The Legion Hall Bombing

Ninety-minute television play.
Transmitted: BBC1, 22 Aug. 1978 (dir. Roland Joffe; with Niall Toibin
as the Defence Counsel).

Unpublished, but the original prologue and epilogue, removed by the
BBC, are in Catherine Itzin, *Stages in the Revolution*, p. 280-1.

*The only documentary play I've done was a television play
about Northern Ireland, about a trial in the Diplock courts,
which were introduced in 1973 because the government felt it
was too hard to get convictions otherwise. There's no jury and
only one judge. I had the transcript of a trial of a boy who was
given sixteen years. A bomb had been planted in a British
Legion Hall where some people were playing cards, and a boy
walked in, put the thing down, and said, 'Clear the hall' and
they all went out. Half an hour later, a small bomb went off and
nobody was hurt. The trial was extraordinary because there was
no evidence to say the boy who was accused did it, except the
police saying he'd confessed, which he denied. There was no
signed statement by him. And there was an old man who'd been
in the hall who said, 'I don't know what boy it was but it was
definitely not* that *boy.' There was no positive identification at
all, and it was hard to believe you would get a conviction in a
normal court. So I did a play for television with Roland Joffe; it
meant reducing the nine and a half hours of trial transcript. We
put on a voice-over at the beginning and end of the programme
that explained the Diplock courts, and the BBC took it off
because they said it was political comment, and put one of their
own in different words, which they said was objective. We took
our names off the credits as a protest.*

Churchill, interviewed by Emily Mann in
Interviews with Contemporary Women Playwrights,
eds. Kathleen Betsko and Rachel Koenig (New York:
Beech Tree Books, 1987), p. 81

The original commentary was dubbed on in March 1978 and nothing
was said about it being unacceptable.

On 19 July a memo was sent to the director and the producer
[Margaret Matheson] asking them to redub the commentary as a result of
discussion with Controller Northern Ireland and the Director of News
and Current Affairs. Several cuts and changes were asked for in the first
paragraph and the second was to be deleted completely 'as we anticipate
this will be covered by the discussion afterwards'. James Cellan-Jones,
Head of Plays, did not give specific reasons for the particular changes,

but said that the commentary would be seen by the viewer as the BBC's editorial comment. I replied suggesting that the BBC could make a disclaimer pointing out that the commentary expressed the viewpoint of the makers of the play; he replied that this would be 'a shabby cop-out'.

On 10 August I learned that there was to be no discussion programme although the discussion programme had been given as a justification for removing the entire final half of the commentary; and that the BBC had now completely removed the commentary to replace it with one of their own. . . .

Our intentions in making the play were clear to the BBC from early on. We researched the material thoroughly and are confident that our commentary is accurate and responsible. The BBC have not banned this play but they have distorted it so that its meaning is changed. This kind of censorship is more subtle and more dangerous than simply banning plays.

Churchill, from unpublished notes written in 1978

Untitled

Written: 1978.

Valery, who had the power to make objects levitate, loses her power.

Cloud Nine

Play in two acts.
Written: after a workshop with Joint Stock Theatre Group.
First production: by Joint Stock Theatre Group, first performed
    at Dartington College of Arts, 14 Feb. 1979, then on tour; first
    performed in London at the Royal Court Th., 27 Mar. 1979
    (dir. Max Stafford-Clark; des. Peter Hartwell; music Andy Roberts;
    with Julie Covington, Carole Hayman, Jim Hooper, William Hoyland,
    Mirian Margolyes, Tony Rohr and Antony Sher).
First New York production: Lucille Lortel's Th. de Lys, 18 May 1981
    (dir. Tommy Tune; des. Lawrence Miller; with E. Katherine Kerr,
    Zeljko Ivanek and Concetta Tomei).
Revived: Royal Court Th., 4 Sept. 1980 (dir. Max Stafford-Clark
    and Les Waters; with Ron Cook, Hugh Fraser, Graeme Garden,

Anna Nygh, Anthony O'Donnell, Maggie Steed and Harriet Walter);
Latchmere Th., 10 Feb. 1986 (dir. Chris Fisher; des. Suzanne
Glanister; with Helen Copp, Sara Coward, Jeffrey Daunton,
Beverley Foster, James Mansfield, Chris Matthews and
Anthony Smee).

Published: London: Pluto Press and Joint Stock Theatre Group, 1979,
revised 1984; and in *Plays: One.*

*Act One takes place in British Imperial Africa in the 1870s,
where Clive, a colonial administrator, heads his family. Illicit
sexual liaisons abound or are thwarted. Upon discovering his
friend Harry Bagley to be homosexual, Clive insists on his
marrying the governess, Ellen, whom the audience knows to be
lesbian. Betty, Clive's wife, is played by a man; Edward, their
son, is played by a woman; Victoria, their daughter, is played by
a doll; and Joshua, the black servant, is played by a white.
Act Two takes place in a London park in 1979, although for the
characters from Act One it is only twenty-five years later. The
sexual liaisons continue to abound, but with less repression and
guilt. Betty, now divorced from Clive and living alone, embraces
the ghost of herself from Act One. The only cross-playing in this
act is of Cathy, a child, who is played by a man.*

By mismatching the performers with their stage roles, Churchill under-
scores the artificiality and conventionality of the characters' sex roles. A
clever theatrical idea thus serves a dramatic purpose, and the sexual
shenanigans that result give rise to more than just the predictable cheap
laughs. When Bagley reveals himself to be riotously polymorphous in
his perversity, for example, we are constantly nudged off balance as we
watch his simultaneously risible and alarming advances toward Betty,
Edward, Joshua and even Clive. . . . Our repugnance toward Harry's
pederastic involvement with Edward, for example, is given a twist by
our recognition that the latter is played by a young woman, just as our
amusement at Harry's adulterous liaison with Betty is skewed by our
knowledge that the latter is played by a young man. Likewise, when the
timid Edward finally shows some spunk by dressing down Joshua, his
mother cheers, . . . while we are plunged into a jungle of conflicting
feelings about what it means for a 'boy' (with the quotation marks very
much supplied by the casting) to become a man, when masculinity is
defined in terms of sexual as well as racial superiority.

Robert Asahina, *The Hudson Review*, XXXIV (1981), p. 565

Cloud Nine is full of good lines and effective little situations; but at the end of it I felt we had seen nothing more than an enjoyable exhibition of the splendid acting of the Joint Stock Theatre Group.

The play is in two distinct halves. The first employs all the current disparaging ideas about the colonial era. It is as ill-informed as it is ill-natured, but neither characteristic matters much, since it takes the form of a cartoon in which historical accuracy is not essential. . . .

Should we learn something from the comparison of the two worlds? I learnt nothing, I'm afraid. . . . If the aim is to show, as the theme song suggests, that any kind of sexual union may be blissful, this is old news by now.

B. A. Young, *Financial Times*, 30 Mar. 1979

Though Caryl Churchill's . . . prose is very often witty, the play falters whenever the jokes run out. . . .

[In Act One] we get the message — we get it, in fact, within seconds of the curtain rising; we are these people's heirs, their repressions ours. They make occasional spectral appearances in Act Two, which is set here and now, but since they were never really alive in the first place, it is difficult to attach much importance to their ghosts. They spoil what is otherwise a far more considerable achievement; this second half is almost the best thing to arrive in the London theatre this young and dismal year. Dealing with people they know and understand, the show's creators begin to do themselves justice.

Robert Cushman, 'That Old Sex Warp', *The Observer*, 1 Apr. 1979

I am . . . sorry that Ms. Churchill's play opts not for a detailed exploration of one area but for a frivolously superficial jog around the whole complex and fascinating territory of sexual relations.

Michael Billington, *The Guardian*, 30 Mar. 1979

It is a fine piece richly deserving its present revival, but I think Miss Churchill disregards the crude facts of audience psychology by starting the evening with some uproariously coarse jokes at the expense of Victorian pieties, and then modulating into something altogether gentler and non-satirical. Long into last night's second half, there were uneasy giggles from spectators trying to view a study in sexual evolution as if it were another ludicrous chapter in the history of the White Man's Burden. . . .

Beyond the laughs, the real dramatic interest lies in the double approach to character as a fixed or fluid thing. The triumph of the play, and of Max Stafford-Clark's production, is that this point is inscribed in the casting.

Irving Wardle, *The Times*, 10 Sept. 1980

What binds the two halves is the tone of the writing, which is compassionate, witty and economic. There is no straining after period effects in Africa: just an attempt to make every line count and to reveal character development through a series of snapshot encounters. . . .

Flip and relaxed in the nicest middle-class manner, the evening amounts to an impressively adult entertainment.

Michael Coveney, *Financial Times*, 5 Sept. 1980

The ideology of the Victorian family is shown to interweave class and male superiority, and hence to suppress female sexuality and homosexuality. The speed and wit reinforce the tightness of the structures within which they all live, and weld form and content into a very clear socialist-feminist perspective, linking the macro-political dynamic (the public) with the micro-political (the personal). . . . The second half is merely a series of isolated portraits of more libertarian sexual relationships in the 1970s, with no sense of how or why they might link with macro-political ideology. The dynamic, therefore, as far as the women were concerned . . . is to present us with a series of individualized bourgeois feminist life-styles from whom the puritanical constraints of Victorian ideology appear to have been lifted. This implies that while we can analyze the past, we cannot analyze the present, and this actually diminishes the potential of the bourgeois feminist dynamic. We don't even get any sense of struggle from the characters; they simply 'are' different, implying that anyone who wants to can simply 'be' different.

Michelene Wandor, 'The Fifth Column: Feminism and Theatre',
Drama, No. 152 (1984), p. 7

[In New York, *Cloud Nine*] was broader, so it was more farcical in the first act and more emotional in the second. Tommy [Tune] talked about 'permission to laugh' and thought the American audience might not realize at the beginning of the play that it was meant to be funny if the colonial thing was played as straight as it had been in England. And the other difference — which ties in with the more emotional feeling of the second half — is the moving of Betty's monologue and the song to the end of the play, to make more of a climax. It was sort of wonderful — the emotion at the end of the play in the American production — but I

43

didn't really like it as much because it threw so much emphasis onto Betty as an individual, while the other way seemed to be more about the development of a group of people, in the same way as the first act. The New York version also meant that it ended with her very solitary, having the self-discovery that she enjoys sex in masturbation, but without taking her on from that to anything else. Whereas that monologue originally came earlier in the scene, so you know from that that she's a sexual person and then you see her make her first move out toward someone else, even though it's a completely ridiculous and wrong move, trying to pick up her son's gay lover, but you know she'll have another go another time and it will work. . . .

In the original production there's a song before the last scene of the second act and it's as if during it things change, because in the last scene everyone has moved on a bit and things have got better. But Tommy felt having the music there would make people think that was the ending, because we had a sort of climax with the music and then the last scene where people had changed and it ended more levelly and coolly. He wanted a different song, more uplifting, whereas the original one was a bit more ironic, and he wanted the music and climax right at the end. So it had quite a different shape and feeling to it. . . .

They took it more to an emotional, personal point. . . . This is one of the differences between the work that comes out of a company like Joint Stock, which tends to deal more with groups of people and society as opposed to the personal.

> Churchill, interviewed by Emily Mann, in
> *Interviews with Contemporary Women Playwrights*,
> ed. Kathleen Betsko and Rachel Koenig, p. 83-4

The two distinct acts of *Cloud Nine* invite the audience to examine their own moral and sexual codes. The fullness of these issues depends on the retrospective interplay between the two acts, and Tune's direction does not do full justice to Churchill's complexity. As a director whose training has been in American musical comedy, Tune seems ill-equipped to bring out fully the imaginativeness and commitment of a British fringe writer who challenges our notions of human behaviour.

> Alisa Solomon, *Theatre Journal*, XXXIV, 1 (Mar. 1982), p. 117-8

Working with just the right, delicate balance of rowdiness and sensitivity — as well as with an unusually good cast — Mr. Tune often succeeds in giving a seriously overlong evening the illusion of flight.

> Frank Rich, 'Sexual Confusion on *Cloud Nine*',
> *The New York Times,* 20 May 1981

Although Act One is a caricature of the world we grew up in, Churchill's first somersault is the one that shows us what we couldn't really have been aware of as children. Namely, that no matter how much our fathers and our 'great white fathers' insisted on creating and observing the rules of civilization, they could do nothing to stem the onrush of human instincts. And then perhaps some of those rules weren't so healthy anyway: because the masks they forced upon people — particularly women and others without power — robbed them of their identities. Those without power had to *become* the roles that their great white father dictated for them. The world we see in Act One is one in which the mask of rightness fashioned by fathers through history has been worn for so long that everyone has lost touch with his essential human needs, with the result that those needs now rush on out of control. . . .

[In Act Two], suddenly, the rules of Act One don't apply any more; in fact the embodier of those rules, the father, has all but disappeared from the stage. People aren't wearing ill-suited masks any longer, but they haven't quite figured out what to do with what they are finding underneath those rejected masks. The characters in Act Two are adults in a world for which their childhoods never prepared them; a world whose fluidity and seeming disorder are both exhilarating and disorienting.

> John Glore, programme note to production at Arena Stage,
> Washington, 5 Apr. 1984 (dir. Gary Pearle)

Caryl Churchill's *Cloud Nine* . . . says something interesting about how the artistic vehicle (here, the shape of the play) relates to what it is trying to tell us. . . .

The biggest difference between the first and second acts is that a production which started out amusing greatly has become attenuated and full of quiet anguish, with play and players pulled in all directions at once.

Miss Churchill's point seems to be that while sexual liberation, so-called, has not been without sad losses, it has yet resulted in new freedoms worth having. The trouble with this, from the playgoer's standpoint, is that the first act was, compared to the second one, *much more fun.*

> Editorial, 'Silver Lining',
> *The Washington Times*, 1 May 1984

The impossibility of the 'women's position' — guilty for being both too strong and too weak — is underlined with passion, frustration and, thankfully, ambiguity.

> Sheila Fox, *City Limits*, 14 Feb. 1986

Where once the 'African' act drew disturbing resonances from its voyage into 'dark, female lust', there now seems — to a post-Boy George generation — echoes of Cooney rather than Conrad; where once the second 'Clapham Junction' act brimmed with possibilities as gender boundaries dissolved, there now seems an unresolved mess which could be dubbed 'Six Characters in Search of a Decent Fuck'. Time, I think, will put this play in its right perspective.

Christine Eccles, *Time Out*, 13 Feb. 1986

The workshops begin. They consist of an open and varied set of explorations. The company invite people in to talk to the group (feminist historian Sheila Rowbotham, Julie [Covington]'s mum, the woman caretaker of the rehearsal rooms); they do improvisations on sexual status and confidence — for example, people choose a card and if it has a high number have to play high sexual confidence in a scene. The individual roles of writer, director and performer are deliberately blurred to maximize participation; everyone is free to suggest and initiate areas of work, books to read, ideas to discuss. The workshops have two inter-related functions: to establish a good working relationship between members of the company, and to provide the mass of 'raw material' which Caryl will draw on to write the play.

Michelene Wandor, 'Free Collective Bargaining', *Time Out*, 30. Mar.-4 Apr. 1979, p. 14

Its title comes from the way one of the older women who came to talk to the company described orgasm.

Michelene Wandor, as above, p. 15

[I have] never felt so close to a play. It is like a second skin.

Jim Hooper, quoted in Michelene Wandor, as above, p. 16

We explored Genet's idea that colonial oppression and sexual oppression are similar. And we explored the femininity of the colonized person. We looked at England's relation to Ireland and how it is like a male/female relationship. The traditional view of the Irish is that they're charming, irresponsible, close to nature, all the things that people tend to think about women.

Churchill, interviewed by John Simon, in 'Sex, Politics, and Other Play Things', *Vogue*, Aug. 1983, p. 126, 130

[I wanted] a sort of speedy, brightly coloured first act, structured as a conventional dramatic experience, and dominated by men. I then wanted the second act to be dominated by women and gays and change, and to be unsettling — not to meet the audience's expectations. To catch them offguard. The second act was originally going to consist entirely of monologues.

Churchill, quoted in Judith Thurman,
'Caryl Churchill: the Playwright who Makes You Laugh about Orgasm,
Racism, Class Struggle,
Homophobia, Woman-Hating, the British Empire,
and the Irrepressible Strangeness of the Human Heart',
Ms, May 1982, p. 56

Rehearsing the first act of *Cloud Nine* when we first did it, we thought oh, this is terribly funny, it's like a farce. It was much funnier than I'd realized writing it — I mean it had made me smile, but it hadn't made me fall off my chair at all. Then we rehearsed the seriousness of the relationships and it all became incredibly sad — all these awful betrayals and people who were in love with people who didn't even know they existed — and the whole thing became quite painful. Then we put together the sequence of truthfully played painful love stories and it all became very funny again, and the more funny for being done for real.

Churchill, interviewed by Lynne Truss, in 'A Fair Cop',
Plays and Players, Jan. 1984, p. 9

[Act One] bore no direct resemblance to the workshop which had never dealt specifically with Victorian sexual politics. Caryl had obviously been inspired and nourished by the workshop, but had then taken a bold imaginative leap and used a different period and society to highlight the themes of sexual prejudice and role-playing.

Antony Sher, in *The Joint Stock Book*, ed. Rob Ritchie,
(London: Methuen, 1987), p. 139-42

In *Cloud Nine* having the historical first act wasn't so much to have a background scene saying 'this is how we came to be as we are'; it was more in order to show the sorts of changes that people even now felt they'd had to make. When we discussed our backgrounds it occurred to us it was as if everyone felt they had been born almost in the Victorian age. Everyone had grown up with quite conventional and old-fashioned expectations about sex and marriage and felt that they themselves had

had to make enormous break-aways and leaps to change their lives from that. That was why it was an appropriate image for that to set the people's childhoods in Victorian times.

Churchill, interviewed by Lynne Truss, as above, p. 10

What is important . . . is that the feelings and characters of the first act should be played for real, so that we do care about them as people. Otherwise the second act loses out too — you have for instance to care about Betty in Act One to care about her properly in Act Two, and so on. And of course if the first act does just go as farce it's for one thing not a very good farce and for another sets up expectations of a kind of entertainment that aren't met in the second act. It's important from the beginning the audience realize what kind of thing they have to pay attention to, and that is essentially the same throughout the play — the relationships between the characters, their relationship to their society, the pain and humour that come out of that. . . .

The first act obviously isn't naturalistic but should be played for real; the second act clearly gets played for real but mustn't get naturalistic. Cathy helps that, of course. . . . There [is] . . . a danger . . . of Act Two all flowing together so much that the stages of each scene [aren't] . . . clear. There's the first scene that mainly gets the characters introduced. There's the long scene a couple of months later going from the first Edward and Gerry through to 'I think I'm a lesbian', the scene where basically the women (or the female side of things, whatever, including Edward) are having a bad time, and Betty, Vic and Edward are all still very neurotic and uptight from their legacy from Act One. Then there's the goddess scene, midsummer or so by now, when the women assert themselves, magic happens, ghosts start to be laid, ending with little Edward and Gerry. Then there's the final scene, late summer, when everyone has to some extent been changed. . . . The original 'Cloud Nine' song coming before the last scene, after the goddess scene, helped mark the change; though there was the danger of a false climax . . . it did mark a turning point and make the final scene clearly something different. . . .

It might be useful to take the characters one by one.

Clive has to run the first act with his energy. It's the male, patriarchal, heterosexual, empire building act with a galloping plot, and a lot of it is to do with him trying to keep together his world, which is starting to crumble at the beginning with murmurings among the natives and Harry's arrival, and is in pieces by the end. Originally I wrote it with a small man in mind, an indoor man, an administrator, a little Napoleon without much natural authority, just the authority of his position. Harry by contrast was glamorous. . . . What is important is to see his increasing desperation. At the beginning he is confidently managing the rivalry between Betty and Joshua, by the end he is hastily scrabbling together a marriage that he knows is a sham. He is probably very drunk in the last scene. He is pretending to believe in what is happening; nobody else is, except Maud, who probably does. He has confidently introduced us to his world at the beginning — by the end nobody in it is what he wants them to be. As the play goes on he more and more obviously seizes on excuses for Edward — the first time with the doll is relatively straightforward, the second time in the beating scene he has for a moment to search more urgently for a reason that makes Edward's behaviour manly, the final time with the necklace it is part of the desperate sham of that whole last scene.

Betty. The pitfalls are . . . obvious. . . . If the actor just plays that person in that situation and doesn't worry about playing a woman, it will probably be fine. There are moments when she is more affected than others, like the love scene with Harry (though even that can be played straighter than you might think, the words do a lot without the actors needing to comment much) and there are moments when she can be really strong and forceful, with all the force of the male actor, like when she tells Joshua to go back to the house or hurls herself at Mrs. Saunders. That really should be a proper physical attack, a real rugby tackle that brings Mrs. Saunders to the ground. . . . Mrs. Saunders needless to say barely defends herself, the attack is all Betty's. There is nothing particularly weak, poetic, hysterical about Betty, only about Clive's image of her. She throws and catches balls excellently.

Edward changes a lot through the act. He shouldn't be too odd a child. . . . He'd be fine if Clive didn't want him to be something different. He starts out the act innocent and ends quite corrupt and devious. The excuses for the doll start impulsively, and become far more conscious. By the time of the necklace excuse in the last scene, it is quite calculated and plays on what he knows Clive will be looking for. He really loves Harry and is really betrayed. By the end of the act he is well set up to be the uptight, repressed, anxious Edward of the beginning of Act Two.

Joshua. Extremely important obviously that he's white and not in black face. He's a white like Betty's a man. Also important that he is genuinely and totally devoted to Clive all the way through. . . . He [sings] . . . 'In the deep midwinter', and nobody else [sings] . . . at all — it [is] . . . a performance for the master by someone totally alienated from his own culture singing about snow that he'd never seen. . . . He is completely devoted to Clive in and through the killing of his parents (though obviously still partly of his own world in putting earth on his head). It is only when Clive turns on him — get out of my sight — that he flips.

Maud. Not much of a problem. A strong woman in a dependent position.

Ellen. A clergyman's daughter? Anyway someone who has to have a job and is doing this not because she likes children but because going to Africa seemed a bit of an adventure. At first she just has a crush on Betty I think, and doesn't really know what she feels. There is . . . the difference in attitude to female and male homosexuality for Victorians — male was reviled etc. *à la* Oscar Wilde and Clive-Harry; female was invisible — like Queen Victoria not knowing it existed so they couldn't pass a law against it because it would mean explaining it to her, and the generally accepted lovingness both in words and physicalness between women without anyone thinking it sexual, so that in general it was invisible. It's invisible to Betty obviously — she doesn't realize ever, even when Ellen is declaring her love so directly at the end. . . . It seems important that her own feelings are at first invisible even to Ellen — the scene of touching hair etc. should be a discovery for her, rather than a lewd seizing of an opportunity. She realizes her passion more as the scene goes on, and has progressed to being really in love by the time of the 'I'd rather die than leave you' etc. She is shattered by the totalness of rejection and misunderstanding, and 'What if I said yes' is genuine wondering, not an acceptance; it is Clive who rushes it into being that. It's a sad character and only comic after that and because of it; absolutely not a sly lewd pantomime maid.

Mrs. Saunders. She's a strong woman who has been running a farm alone since her husband died. She's fairly humanitarian, doesn't let the servants be beaten etc. Without putting her ahead of her time she's more aware of what's happening and more progressive than the others. (Or maybe it's better to see both her and Harry, the outsiders to the family who can't possibly fit it or the society, as similar in this.) She genuinely comes to Clive for safety not sex. She sleeps with him when he comes to her bed the first night, out of relief at safety, physical comfort, and indeed sex, but that doesn't mean she wants that to be the terms of their relationship. She absolutely is not flirting with him during the 'why ride off now' scene, but is really trying to explain her position. In the end it is sheer physical sensation that takes over briefly. . . . She does enjoy it briefly, is indignant when it stops. She's a rather brisk horsey woman. . . . The main point about her is that she's an independent woman, and that Clive interprets her being on her own as making her a seductress. Key lines for her are 'There's no place for me here', and 'I shall keep leaving everywhere I suppose'.

Harry. He's a homosexual, genuinely in love with Edward. His betrayal of Edward is serious and appalling to them both. He does idolize Betty, as a good woman, a mother, etc., and rather likes the idea of being her unrequited lover, a far more acceptable role than admitting what he is. When she wants more than that, he at once retreats and tries hard to keep her where she is. Joshua is casual and direct sex by contrast with the romancing Betty. The love scene with Edward can be quite a straight love scene. The crocodile story . . . should have sexual implications but quite veiled for both of them and should really be about the pleasure of being alone together at last. In so far as there's physical contact and rolling around together (if that's even necessary which I doubt) it should be something they can both take as innocent and within their uncle relationship and which only helps lead on to something else rather than pre-empting it. This is quite important. Harry is quite shattered and defeated by the end of the play and not putting a particularly good face on it. He makes a feeble attempt to go back to his old chatting up line with Betty, which she slaps down — I shall get drunk. He is still in love with Edward, though pretending now entirely to be the adult and uncle.

Act Two. The main thing about the characters is that they all change, slightly. Betty, Edward and Vic bring the tensions and repressions of the first act with them. Simplistically, they are changed by Lin and Gerry (who are both homosexual and working class, which may be relevant). The changes aren't to some idyllic and happy end obviously, but everyone has got a bit less rigid and more open.

Betty. The stages she goes through should be quite distinct. In the first scene she has just taken, is just taking, the decision to leave Clive. (Maybe she doesn't even know it as definite until she's said it, like 'There I've said it, it's true', in the first act.) She has to run the first scene off her hysteria and leave Cathy hysterical. She is avoiding contact with her children. In the next scene she's left him, is living alone in a flat, depends a lot on Vic and Martin. She's in a near breakdown state of panic and agoraphobia, acute anxiety. She is beginning to relate to people a bit though, expecially Lin. Then there's the scene she's not in, the magic or whatever scene. When we next see her she's changed a lot. She still chats on a lot and has moments of not being able to face what's happening but she is basically okay and setting off on her new life. . . . She is the same person as Act One Betty and it can help if both actors are aware of that (similarly with Edward) not just as a fact because it's obvious but as something to think about, for the Act Two characters to be aware of where they've come from. A useful key to Betty is 'I want to be dangerous'. It's something that makes the double with Gerry nice — there's a shadow there somewhere of Betty being dangerous, and it has reverberations for their scene together.

Edward. Not usually a problem, so long as he's sufficiently uptight and even a touch camp at the beginning to give himself somewhere to change from. Actors are usually (rightly) so wary of making him any kind of stage faggot that they end up playing him the same all through.

There does have to be reason enough for Gerry to say 'Just be yourself'. It does have to be clear that it is Edward who is making the relationship neurotic, that he is trying to change Gerry into something he isn't and can't be. The change for Edward is from having rejected being a man if it means being like Clive and taken instead the idea of being a woman but with his only model for that Betty from Act One, to realizing through Vic and Lin that being a woman isn't some special stereotyped way of behaving so that he can just be himself, do the things he likes, look after Cathy or whatever without feeling there's a whole old-fashioned feminine behaviour that goes with that. So that by the time he meeets Gerry again he's still doing housework etc. etc. and still identifying strongly with women, but in a quite different way which makes him more relaxed, more able to relate properly to Gerry as whatever Gerry is rather than as raw material for a husband fantasy.

Gerry. Originally Gerry's monologue was at the beginning . . . and it was a nice jolt to start the act as clearly somewhere very different. But it gave the audiences a fright and turned them against Gerry, who seemed just the sort of horrible maniac they hoped they'd never meet on a train, which was not the intention. By moving it to after the scene with Edward (this was in England after about a week of touring) it made people more on Gerry's side and able to go off and enjoy the adventure with him. Gerry can be older than Edward as he was originally, or younger . . . that's quite nice as it makes Edward's fantasy of being the wife even more obviously inappropriate. What's important I think is that he's nice, not particularly fucked up. He does love Edward and he does also enjoy promiscuity. He genuinely likes being alone, that's not just defensive, but the change he goes through (not a major one, Edward changes more) is realizing how much he loves and depends on Edward and would like to get back to him. . . . Somehow [the appearance of young Edward's ghost] . . . and Gerry picking up Harry (. . . no need for the ghosts just to flit across the back, they can walk around quite solidly like anyone else in the park) should lay those ghosts, and the love between Gerry and Edward make up for the hurt of the destruction of Harry and Edward's love. It seems to me really good that the person Betty tries to chat up is Gerry and that he's nice to her, etc., and that that should be the last scene as she reaches out for the first time.

Vic. Fairly clear I think. Goes from the little doll of Act One to someone who still finds it hard to be seen rather than heard, can't talk to Martin etc. Her feminism and politics is all in books and the head and it takes her relationship with Lin to loosen it up and make it real. So what happens to her is that change, to something less uptight, more feeling.

Martin. . . . He, like Vic, has all his sexual politics in the head, doesn't mean harm, means quite well with nasty flashes, but is so used to being in charge that he finds it hard to stop and talks Vic into the ground with what is meant to be the politics of her freedom. One of the things Act Two is about is how hard it is to give up power (for men, for Britain in Ireland) as well as how hard it is to take freedom. Martin has all the theory of having given it up while keeping it in practice. The change for him is that he does begin to talk less and do more, goes from not speaking to Lin to looking after her child, from theorizing about a different form of life to trying to live one. The row with Lin was so as not to make him too perfect or make it seem too easy; and a row is still better than refusing to speak at all. Then the actor originally playing him wanted something to get sympathy back in case he'd lost it by shouting so we put in the bit about holding Tommy on the sofa. . . . For me the moment I used to feel sorriest for him . . . was when the other three went off — tell me when you're sober. He and Vic are still fond of each other at the end. Who if anyone is going to go on having what relationship with whom is left completely unsettled.

Lin seems easy enough. . . . It's important she should be warm. She (like Gerry) changes less than the others, but she does get a bit of theory from Vic perhaps, and gets less hostile to men, through Edward and then Martin, who she may have a row with but basically has some kind of working relationship with by the end. She's important to Betty too.

Cathy seems to be better the more closely the actor observes four to five year old girls and the less he relies on some fantasy of what they might be. She's not a horrible child. . . . The theory of her being played by a man . . . is partly just a reversal of the more conventional woman-plays-boy from Act One; partly I suppose it throws up more clearly the extent to which behaving like a proper little girl is learnt rather than innate; partly that the emotional size and force of a small child in a group is better represented on stage by a large and forceful man than it would be by a child. . . . Cathy's change — from being whining and overdependent on Lin to relating to all of them, I suppose. And the negative change by the second scene where she's more conscious of trying to be a proper little girl. I don't think she changes in the sense Betty, Vic, Edward, Martin or even Gerry and Lin do, though.

The Soldier. . . . The last bit of empire, 'fucking' as sex and aggression, a man's life, his anger and pain at what he's been through, and real yearning for something else at the end.

The goddess scene needs to build quite lightly and quickly up through that chanting, the audience needs to be possibly deceived by what Lin sees because for all it knows something will appear, the play might be making a move into the supernatural then rather than a few moments later. Then it turns out to be a joke, to be back to reality and fooling around in the park, then it turns out real magic has somehow started. The soldier needn't just appear at the back in a puff of smoke, he can quite concretely walk on and be like a real person if you prefer. I rather like solid ghosts myself.

> Churchill, unpublished letter to Richard Seyd
> during rehearsals for his production of *Cloud Nine*,
> Eureka Theater Company, San Francisco, 10 May 1983

Three More Sleepless Nights

Play in three scenes.
First London production: Soho Poly Th., 9 June 1980; trans. to
   Royal Court Th. Upstairs, 5 Aug. 1980 (dir. Les Waters; with
   Jan Chappell as Margaret, Fred Pearson as Frank, Kevin McNally as
   Pete, and Harriet Walter as Dawn).

The three sleepless nights are three scenes in a bed, first with a verbose married couple in their tenth year of warfare, then with a second muted couple, the woman pushing to grief and suicide, the man describing the plot of the film Alien. *A minor shuffle takes place for the third night, with the obsessively jealous wife and the film-going catatonic forming a new couple, beginning with cheer and self-congratulations and finding their way back to the patterns that served them before.*

Stated baldly, it sounds obvious, but Miss Churchill's writing has enough energy to make it intriguing and Les Waters has directed it with a great deal of additional energy. The first scene is played as fast as a slap to the face and the second rolls quietly towards death.

> Ned Chaillet,
> *The Times*, 11 June 1980

This is what happens when a place flatters itself that it is a 'writers' theatre'. Caryl Churchill writes good dialogue, creates good characters, understands the tensions that build up in bedrooms. Any of these three scenes would make an effective quarter-hour passage in a play. As self-contained entertainment, they are no more than scribbles in a note pad.

Certainly in an ideal world there should be a place where writers could see their exercises produced; but it's asking rather a lot to charge the public to see them.

> B. A. Young,
> *Financial Times*, 6 Aug. 1980

The piece . . . is too inconsequential to give more than momentary pleasure. It lacks punch, which its form implies, and the dramatic intensity of its Strindbergian echoes. . . .

At least the show is brief. It is all over in an hour.

Eric Shorter, 'Signs All Couples Will Recognize',
Daily Telegraph, 6 Aug. 1980

Crimes

One-hour television play.
Transmitted: BBC 1, 13 Apr. 1982 (dir. Stuart Burge;
with Sylvestra le Touzel as Jane and T. P. McKenna as Melvyn).

Caryl Churchill's Play for Tomorrow, Crimes, *was an anthology of human wrongdoing, connected by an alienatingly perfunctory narrative. A videotape of an interview is shown to a group of prisoners; their reactions and a subsequent discussion are recorded on a further tape which the prison administrator watches at home in his shelter. The crimes are not so much compared as juxtaposed. The play's separate elements merge only in the mind of the viewer, who is left to place the characters in some hierarchy of relative guilt. . . .*

The play, directed with uncompromising harshness by Stuart Burge, focused on individual cases to demonstrate the possibility of defining crime. Sylvestra le Touzel gave a fascinatingly cool performance as the sweet, neat teenage mass murderer. Peter Whitbread was quietly desperate as a nature-lover in a world where even wood-lice were extinct. T. P. McKenna looked sinisterly pasty-faced as the man responsible for implanting an electrode in the girl-killer's brain. . . .

All law-breaking, argued a black prisoner, is a form of political protest. Behind all these individual crimes, Churchill seemed to suggest in this complex and interesting play, lay a far greater one, the act of collective vandalism which was creating that inhuman society.

Lucy Hughes-Hallett, 'Hierarchy of Relative Guilt',
The Times, 14 Apr. 1982

It was a grimly persuasive piece, with a mesmerizingly sinister performance from Sylvestra le Touzel. I say performance, which suggests something dramatic. Actually, *Crimes* was a series of hideously effective monologues built around a minimum of action: it bore the same relation to a play as an oratorio does to an opera.

John Peter, 'Dallas: the Lure of a Never-Never Land',
Sunday Times, 18 Apr. 1982

The . . . play was poorly served by a dreadfully tedious style of direction (which may even have been inspired by the writer, who knows) in which cameras move as little as possible, especially during long monologues.

Chris Dunkley, 'Vexed Issues', *Financial Times*, 21 Apr. 1982

She has really written four monologues, dense with absorbing ideas on tomorrow's attitudes to crime and criminals, but self-contained and therefore armoured against dramatic change. . . .

Within its own demanding terms, the piece is ingeniously constructed, revealing itself like the layers of an onion, and directed with a meticulous eye by Stuart Burge.

Sean Day-Lewis, 'Plays for Tomorrow', *Daily Telegraph*, 14 Apr. 1982

Caryl Churchill has a long apprenticeship in radio and no one told her you could not write long, marvellous monologues, great lava streams of torrential talk, for TV. So she wrote them. We learn about Britain in 2002 by inference, in the sparks from these speeches.

Nancy Banks-Smith, 'Future Shock', *The Guardian*, 14 Apr. 1982

Top Girls

Play in two acts.
First London production: Royal Court Th., 28 Aug. 1982
    (dir. Max Stafford-Clark; des. Peter Hartwell; with Selina Cadell,
    Lindsay Duncan, Deborah Findlay, Carole Hayman, Lesley Manville,
    Gwen Taylor and Lou Wakefield); trans. Joseph Papp's Public Th. at
    the Newman Th., New York, 21 Dec. 1982; returned Royal Court Th.,
    4 Feb. 1983.
First New York production: Joseph Papp's Public Th. at the
    Newman Th., 24 Feb. 1983 (dir. Max Stafford-Clark;
    des. Peter Hartwell; with Sara Botsford, Donna Bullock,
    Kathryn Grody, Lise Hilboldt, Linda Hunt, Valerie Mahaffey and
    Freda Foh Shen).
Published: London: Methuen, 1982; revised edition 1984.

In the first scene Marlene celebrates her promotion to managing director of the Top Girls employment agency. Her dinner guests are five women from history, literature, and art. The rest of the play shows scenes of Marlene's workplace and of the home of her working-class sister, Joyce. Marlene dismisses as a no-hoper her 'niece' Angie, whom the last scene reveals to be her daughter.

In this vigorous if untidy parable for Thatcher's Britain, Caryl Churchill begins by attacking the prevalent view that any woman worth her salt is perfectly free to become a Top Girl, like our leader, and then deftly shifts her argument to class. Neither the 'Patriarchy v Women' nor the 'Us v Them' theme is, of course, an original one for the modern dramatist; what is distinctive in this play is the linking of the two and the skill with which Churchill manipulates her sparring sisters, Marlene and Joyce, as symbols, while creating entirely credible characters. Their argument in the last scene has all the bleak resonance of cradle-bred rivalry, despite some earlier hints of authorial pamphleteering. . . .

[In the last scene], in an extraordinarily effective piece of dialogue, the characters seem to change places before our eyes; Marlene shouts, weeps, pleads for sympathy and it is Joyce who gains stature by rejecting her sister's wheedling attempts at eliciting a compromise. As we learn that Angie is really Marlene's illegitimate child, so Marlene's success is revealed as hollow, subsidized. Churchill offers us a Hobbesian version of feminist theory in which men's achievement depends on their exploitation of women, and women's on their exploitation of other women. The dark and desolate force of this retrospectively lends the first scene of celebration a considerable pathos; we have to remind ourselves that in the narrative sequence, the success comes later. Marlene, with all the selfish force inherent in natural evolution, has survived and prospered.

> Carol Rumens, 'The Price of Success',
> *Times Literary Supplement*,
> 24 Sept. 1982, p. 1035

Dull Gret doesn't say much. She's the real subversive. She — if you except an even more silent waitress — is the only person present not, by birth or adoption, upper class. . . .

The office is revealing, since not only is Marlene a success herself, but she is in the business of sniffing out success in other people, and of mercilessly weeding out failure. . . .

Marlene declares herself a Thatcherite, which we might have deduced for ourselves. Her sister's political stance comes as a surprise, and seems manufactured for the occasion.

But the play runs thin nowhere else. Thoroughly personal in tone and structure, it manages to be an amazingly full polygonal presentation of a feminist predicament: career-women behaving like career-men. The situation is (mostly) deplored, but sympathy is withheld from no-one. Miss Churchill also does for over-lapping dialogue on stage what Robert Altman has done in the movies.

Robert Cushman, *The Observer*, 5 Sept. 1982

Max Stafford-Clark has directed an inchoate play, seemingly written on the principle 'I don't know what I think until I get it on to paper.'

Francis King, *Sunday Telegraph*, 5 Sept. 1982

One of the questions Caryl Churchill put to her fellow-feminists in *Top Girls* . . . was this. What have you, or indeed anyone, to offer the woman who hasn't the mental wherewithal ever to overtake the men on the promotion ladder, run her own office, jet off to New York for meetings and California for holidays, and do all the greater and lesser things associated with 'making it' in our sabre-toothed society? . . .

It has . . . [an] unusual and arresting point to make: liberation is only a subtler, uglier form of enslavement if women have to maim, mutilate and be-Thatcher themselves in order to achieve it.

Benedict Nightingale, *New Statesman*, 25 Feb. 1983

Overlapping dialogue is a brilliant technical feature of the play, and emerging from the precisely organized cross babble we hear competitive stories of rape, childbirth, transsexual disguise, ambition realized through learning, pregnancy and hunger. . . .

The crux of the play comes at the moment when Joyce asks her, in between gulps of whisky, what chance will her own rather stupid, untalented daughter have in such a cruel world. The human question clouds the issue, and Gwen Taylor as Marlene strikes a very deep chord of confused anguish. The carapace of hard, pragmatic get-up-and-go begins to crack.

A talented cast have a field day, switching from historical stereotype to the modern equivalent. *Top Girls* seems at first to be a piece written on the small scale, but the evening takes flight as great arcs of inter-connecting incident and observation light up the scenario.

Michael Coveney, *Financial Times*, 8 Feb. 1983

Caryl Churchill's first scene is like Shaw on an off-day; but thereafter the work builds to a superb emotion-draining climax that sent me out of the theatre convinced that this is the best British play ever from a woman dramatist. . . .

What I admire most about Ms. Churchill is that she is not afraid of downright passion (the rarest commodity in modern British theatre). Having taken us all round her subject, in the final scene Ms. Churchill gives us an eyeball-to-eyeball confrontation . . . and . . . proves that both sisters are in different ways deprived and that some things are bigger than blood-ties.

> Michael Billington,
> *The Guardian*, 9 Feb. 1983

Caryl Churchill is one of the few playwrights who shake my blimpish conviction that one good story is worth any number of major themes. It is not that she disdains story-telling, but that she makes it carry an astonishing weight of extra cargo, which in her case has the paradoxical effect of lightening the craft rather than sinking it.

Dull Gret and Angie are both played by Carole Hayman, whose marvellously imagined portrait of hopeless yearning and suppressed anger, straining into expression through a heavy body and slow intelligence, is the performance I shall best remember.

> Irving Wardle, 'Churchillian Women',
> *The Times,* 9 Feb. 1983

We're never quite convinced that women's choices are as limited and, in the play's final word, 'frightening' as the stacked case of *Top Girls* suggests. Even in England, one assumes, not every woman must be either an iron maiden or a downtrodden serf.

> Frank Rich, 'Caryl Churchill's *Top Girls*, at the Public',
> *The New York Times*, 29 Dec. 1982

I'd say the play is, among other things, a critique of bourgeois feminism; that the motor of its harshness is compassion; that Churchill writes mothers and children better than anyone around; and that sentimentality has rarely been so remote.

[The] beginning can be parsed a multitude of ways; before its meaning starts to unfold in relationship to the rest of the play, it opens us to particularity and history, the power of individual will and the limits of that power — which can be seized only by living disguised as a man, by leaving one's society, by obeying absolutely, by taking arms and disobeying absolutely. Drastic courses. These characters are parables: in women's history you can't get what you want in an ordinary, simple, humane way, if you want anything much.

Erika Munk, 'Making It', *The Village Voice*, 11 Jan. 1983

I think it's a masterful work, but it is very subtle in its presentation of the central character, Marlene. There are scenes in which the point that Caryl wants to be made must be made, or the entire structure crumbles. A crucial scene in which the audience's view of Marlene begins to turn is the one in which Mrs. Kidd enters. For it to work, your sympathy must lie with Marlene for the bulk of the scene. You must feel that Marlene is defending herself against this awful, old-fashioned, nagging, sick woman who is trying to get her to give up her job; that this awful woman represents everything that is wrong with our sexist society, and that Marlene is standing up to her and defending her rights as a woman. The audience at this point should be cheering Marlene on. The moment when Marlene says, 'Will you please piss off!' is the climax of the scene and we — like Angie, her daughter — are supposed to be completely with Marlene. Then Mrs. Kidd collapses emotionally, and she is absolutely destroyed by what Marlene just said to her. That moment is the first hint that Marlene is not a simple hero. She sacrificed something at that moment. She hurt another human being and enjoyed it. But that's the first moment for the audience in which buzzers should start to go off in their heads: 'Wait a minute. Who is this woman?' It's a tremendously delicate problem to convey that. I've watched the scene performed wrong many times and it destroys the fabric of the text. It destroys the arc. If we miss that moment all we are left with is the apparent transformation of Marlene at the end of the last scene when she suddenly speaks of her support for Reagan and Thatcher. I've seen many audiences respond to Marlene as a hero until the last scene when she brings up Reagan and Thatcher. Then members of the audience say to themselves, 'We don't like Reagan/Thatcher policies. Maybe Marlene is not quite the hero we thought.' It has a pernicious effect. It looks like the politics of the play are imposed upon it, rather than the politics being an integral part of the characters' personalities and backgrounds.

What Caryl is trying to show is that Marlene has constructed a life for her that is internally consistent — and that is what is so scary, not just that she supports Reagan. Rather, that her whole background has led inexorably to her supporting Reagan. If you don't bring out that theme consistently, then the audience is not really challenged to examine their own beliefs. They will simply say, 'Well, I don't support Reagan, so I'm fine'.

Oskar Eustis, interviewed by Mark Bly in
'Dramaturgy at the Eureka', *Theater*, XVII, 3 (1986), p. 11-12

I ask Churchill what she intended, and she says she wanted the play to seem, at first, 'to be celebrating the extraordinary achievements of women. Then it would cut another way and say that this sort of movement is useless if you don't have a socialist perspective on it.' The play came, 'very deeply, out of the climate of having a right-wing woman prime-minister'. And it was 'pushed on . . . by a visit to America about three years ago, where I met several women who were talking about how great it was that women were getting on so well now in American corporations, that there were equal opportunities. And although that's certainly part of feminism, it's not what I think is enough. I'm saying there's no such thing as right-wing feminism. . . .

'I quite deliberately left a hole in the play, rather than giving people a model of what they could be like. I meant the thing that is absent to have a presence in the play. . . . I thought, what the hell; if people can't see the values, I don't want to spell them out.'

Laurie Stone, 'Making Room at the Top',
The Village Voice, XXVIII, 9 (1 Mar. 1983), p. 81

With *Top Girls* for the Royal Court I wasn't thinking in terms of doubling at all. My original idea was to write a play for an enormous number of women, and I . . . wrote a play that had sixteen women's parts in it. When it came to doing it, partly because it was being directed by Max Stafford-Clark who . . . [founded] Joint Stock . . . and likes working in that way, partly financial considerations (. . . no one's going to want to do a play with sixteen actors when they can economize and do it with seven) and partly because it is obviously much more enjoyable for the actors and . . . for the whole feel of a play for it to be done by a company — it did seem to make a lot of sense to do it in that way.

Churchill, interviewed by Lynne Truss, in 'A Fair Cop',
Plays and Players, Jan. 1984, p. 9-10

Another advantage of doubling is that you can have very good actors in even the smallest parts. And another effect of it is that the audience can enjoy the medium and appreciate the theatricality rather than over-identifying with the characters.

Churchill, unpublished interview with Linda Fitzsimmons,
19 Apr. 1988

If you want to bring characters from the past onto the stage then you can do it, without having to find a realistic justification, such as presenting it as Marlene's dream. On stage it is possible for these women to meet and have dinner. In the theatre anything's possible.

Churchill, interviewed by Renate Klett, in
' "Anything's Possible in the Theatre":
Portrait of Author Caryl Churchill',
Theater Heute, Jan. 1984, p. 19

Thatcher had just become Prime Minister; there was talk about whether it was an advance to have a woman prime minister if it was someone with policies like hers. She may be a woman but she isn't a sister, she may be a sister but she isn't a comrade. And, in fact, things have got much worse for women under Thatcher. . . .

A lot of people have latched on to Marlene leaving her child, which interestingly was something that came very late. Originally the idea was just that Marlene was 'writing off' her niece, Angie, because she'd never make it, I didn't yet have the plot idea that Angie was actually Marlene's own child. Of course women are pressured to make choices between working and having children in a way that men aren't, so it *is* relevant, but it isn't the main point of it.

There's another thing that I've recently discovered with productions of *Top Girls*. In Greece, for example, where fewer women go out to work, the attitude from some men seeing it was, apparently, that the women in the play who'd gone out to work weren't very nice, weren't happy, and they abandoned their children. They felt the play was obviously saying women *shouldn't* go out to work — they took it to mean what they were wanting to say about women themselves, which is depressing. . . . Another example of its being open to misunderstanding was a production in Cologne, Germany, where the women characters were played as miserable and quarrelsome and competitive at dinner, and the women in the office were neurotic and incapable. The waitress slunk about in a catsuit like a bunnygirl and Win changed her clothes on stage in the office. It just turned into a complete travesty of what it was supposed to be. So that's the sort of moment when you think you'd rather write novels, because the productions can't be changed.

Churchill, interviewed by the editors, in
Interviews with Contemporary Women Playwrights,
ed. Kathleen Betsko and Rachel Koenig, p. 77-8

For me it's not a question of being true to the work, but rather that political intentions should not simply be turned round the other way; so a committed feminist play should not look like an anti-female work at its premiere in German. . . .

Adler's main interest (but why?) seems to be the denunciation of the characters and no cliché is too stupid for him and no reproach too cheap. In the opening scene he has the women prattling brainlessly on in a light chatty tone. Each of them is just concerned with herself and with outdoing the others — just 'competitors' who don't like each other, just the way it is with women. And then, so it doesn't get boring without men on stage, the barmaid is dressed up in a sexy way, waggles her bottom and is even allowed a hot little solo dance! Then the agency scene: it really tears you up to see just how the women pull each other to pieces (we all know about that: so horrid and mean, behind each others' backs, just so feminine). . . .

Let's say it once more: Caryl Churchill didn't mean all that at all. She drew characters, not cardboard cut-outs, she criticizes the women constructively, whereas Adler's criticism is just reactionary. Where she is revealing complex occurrences, psychologically justified patterns of behaviour, he's happy with a copy of the usual sexism.

Renate Klett, 'Male Execution:
the German Premiere of *Top Girls* in Cologne',
[Schauspielhaus, 26 Nov. 1983, dir. Walter Adler],
Theater Heute, Jan. 1984, p. 23

Would Marlene today [1986] still defend Mrs. Thatcher's policy in the same way or would her attitude be a bit more critical after having experienced Mrs. Thatcher's way of governing?

I'm delighted that Mrs. Thatcher's reputation in Vienna is so low, but unfortunately she does still have supporters here and I think Marlene might well be among them.

Thinking naturalistically about the play: the first scenes should probably be in the early autumn because of the conversation between Joyce and Kit — Kit has just moved up to a new class after the summer holiday and it is the first term Angie hasn't been back at school, bringing home to both Joyce and Angie worries about her future. So if you are doing the play in April this year, that is autumn 1985 and the play's final scene would then be autumn 1984. Though that still doesn't get us back to the earliest days of Thatcherism it is only one year after the second election, and her standing was certainly higher then than now. If Marlene and Joyce's quarrel had been a couple of weeks ago they probably couldn't have avoided mentioning Westlands though by April things may be different again — but in any case that scene is always a year behind 'the present'. I think what they say would still stand up in 1984, though a line like 'I think the eighties are going to be stupendous' couldn't come much later than that. Obviously the effect is slightly different if it is said in 1984 rather than 1980, but I don't think the determined optimism this implies is out of character for Marlene.

Dramatically, considering the effects on the audience of hearing this support for Thatcher at the moment, I think it is still okay. In fact, I quite like the irony. I had never intended them to agree with Marlene's argument after all. I think it would be wrong to show Marlene wavering in her convictions; it is important that she is happy and confident about what she is doing, and the dinner party a year later would confirm to her that her predictions of success were right. And the argument is a drunken one between two angry sisters, not a considered political assessment, and is exaggerated and oversimplified on both sides.

Unpublished correspondence between Churchill and Wolfgang Huber, Dramaturg of Ensemble Th., Vienna, during rehearsals for the Austrian premiere, 2 Apr. 1986 (dir. Peter Gruber)

Angry bombing of Libya. Ashamed to be associated with promoting Britain's image abroad. At least play's anti-Thatcher. Best wishes to company.

Unpublished telegram from Churchill to Ensemble Th., Vienna, during British Week in Vienna, 17 Apr. 1986

Fen

Play in twenty-one scenes.
Written: after workshop with Joint Stock Theatre Group.
First production: by Joint Stock Theatre Group; first performed at the University of Essex Th., 20 Jan. 1983; first performed in London, Almeida Th., 16 Feb. 1983; trans. Joseph Papp's Public Th., LuEsther Hall, New York, 24 May 1983; trans. Royal Court Th., 28 July 1983 (dir. Les Waters; des. Annie Smart; lighting Tom Donnellan; with Linda Bassett, Amelda Brown, Cecily Hobbs, Tricia Kelly, Jennie Stoller, and Bernard Strother).
First New York production: Public Th., New York, 23 Feb. 1984 (dir. Les Waters; with Robin Bartlett, Linda Griffiths, Ellen Parker, Pamela Reed, David Strathairn and Concetta Tomei).
Published: London: Methuen, in association with Joint Stock Theatre Group, 1983; and in *'Softcops' and 'Fen'*, Methuen, 1986.

Caryl Churchill's new play for Joint Stock is strikingly designed by Annie Smart. The lights rise slowly on a human scarecrow clacking a rattle and shrouded in mist. She stands in a field of potatoes. An arena of dank, brown soil is boarded on three sides by solid walls.

A Japanese businessman celebrates the territory as a sound investment and the image cross-fades to a line of women in wellies and headscarves advancing bent double over their crop and chanting the theme of a children's TV show, Trumpton. *These figures are both labourers and children of the village. We are somewhere in East Anglia and a working community is deftly conjured through jagged scenes of domestic crisis, collective memory and childhood nightmare.*

The generations flow into one another: a peasant woman, 150 years old, suddenly turns with angry defiance on the farmer who is selling the land she has nursed; a grandmother reminisces vividly on her ninetieth birthday; the ghosts of sisters, a murdered woman and a labourer superstitiously regarded as being a hermaphrodite, mingle finally in each others' dreams as the fog once more rises.

The playwright pins down her poetic subject matter in dialogue of impressive vigour and economy. The piece may not have the high gloss finish of Miss Churchill's *Cloud Nine* and *Top Girls* — plays with which she has joined the premier league — but it is instinct with a brooding rural atmosphere pierced with nursery rhymes, boggarts and a doomed love affair.

This last involves Val, who is torn between her daughters and the man for whom she has abandoned them. Jennie Stoller conveys the dilemma very well in an eerie night scene that leads to a grim climax. It is remarkable how Val's story carries true tragic weight when it appears to have been coloured in so lightly, and in a play that lasts only ninety minutes. We see her rejected, tentatively joining a hot-gospelling hen party, and then returning to Bernard Strother's equally well realized farm hand.

As the community's security shifts beneath its feet, there are sharp little interludes in the local pub, the village streets and a tenant's cottage. Much of all this is like Edward Bond at his best, and Les Waters's production is fully alive to the ebb and flow.

Michael Coveney, Financial Times, 17 Feb. 1983

[Val] appeals to the sympathies whereas the stepmother aroused hatred. But, in the surrounding context, they are two of a kind: two people who try to make something happen in that bland, impoverished environment which duly takes its revenge on them.

Irving Wardle, 'Desolate Isolation', The Times, 17 Feb. 1983

Apart from a whimsical finale, everything in this play fits, no matter how eccentrically shaped it may seem. Miss Churchill tells us all we need to know; not necessarily, though, all we would like to know. . . .

Six actors play 21 roles, which means restless doubling and no chance to get to know anyone, this last compounded by an ostentatious chastity of outline. The method actually works against a sense of community; there are simply never enough people around.

Robert Cushman, *The Observer*, 20 Feb. 1983

What comes over best is the violence born of repression. Whether killing a sheep, beating a stepchild or murdering a faithless wife, all are desperate attempts to experience a single true feeling.

Rosalind Carne, *Financial Times*, 29 July 1983

[*Fen*] is the most stylistically consistent of Miss Churchill's plays and at times the most off-putting. It is also yet another confirmation that its author possesses one of the boldest theatrical imaginations to emerge in this decade.

Frank Rich, '*Fen*, New Work by Caryl Churchill',
The New York Times, 31 May 1983

The lives of the fenland women in Caryl Churchill's play are as bleak as the terrain, but her writing, sharper and tighter than ever, packs in so much detail and understanding that dreariness itself becomes a tragic drama, filled with all her anger at human waste. . . .

Fresh from its New York run, Les Waters's Joint Stock production is in beautiful condition, crucially precise in this elliptical dialogue. . . .

The cast of six play 22 characters . . . establishing them completely in their few minutes of stage life. Miss Stoller and Bernard Strother make the violent ending both appalling and convincing, and Cecily Hobbs does precisely the same for a macabre family story which, delivered in an unvaryingly placid flow, she makes uproariously funny as well. But (to borrow the style a bit) you all deserved, my sugars, the cheers we gave you on the opening night.

Anthony Masters, *The Times*, 2 Aug. 1983

As with the majority of Joint Stock plays, the play was written after company research and workshops, and this is at times reflected in the structure of the piece — a large number of characters representing as many different types of people as can be crammed in. At times devotion to wide representation feels schematic and undermines the emotional continuity of the piece. . . . That these schematic moments are not too disruptive is due to the extraordinary ensemble work by the company, and the quality of Les Waters's production which achieves a beautiful balance between the spare, simple language and the emotional sub-text of the characters' lives.

There are two main themes: first, that despite changes in the pattern of land ownership (from feudal landlords to multi-national corporations) nothing fundamental has changed in the lives of the farming community; and second, that the constant factor in people's lives is a cultural, emotional poverty that is as dangerous as material poverty.

> Michelene Wandor, *Plays and Players*, Oct. 1983, p. 39-40

We spent two weeks living in a cottage in the Fens, meeting people, and talking about their lives, and then one week in London. That final week we discussed what we'd found out and what we wanted in the play. We talked about anger and deference — anger and violence, caused by hard conditions of work, turned inward to self-mutilation or deflected onto people who weren't responsible for it. We also talked of women's endurance and their pride in hard work. We remembered the gangmaster who told us women were better workers than men. They'd work even with icicles on their faces. We wanted to show women constantly working.

> Churchill, interviewed by Geraldine Cousin in
> 'The Common Imagination and the Individual Voice',
> *New Theatre Quarterly*, IV, 13 (Feb. 1988), p. 6

It's a love story, actually, but the play is also about how these people live. . . .

It's a complicated world, . . . incredibly remote and backward in some ways — in the way the workers are very badly paid and yet still feel loyal to the farmers, at the same time that it's entirely of the present, because the land they're loyal to is owned by multinational corporations. The English have an idea that the real England is the countryside, and that it's a beautiful retreat, completely separate from the corrupt values of people living in cities . . . . But it's a pastoral fantasy.

> Churchill, interviewed by Laurie Stone in 'Making Room at the Top',
> *The Village Voice*, XXVIII, 9 (1 Mar. 1983), p. 80

Fen is the most documentary of the plays, I suppose. . . . I was left [after the workshop] with a lot of notes and quotes and things different people had said. But never a whole speech, just lines here and there. And I didn't make any characters who were based on a single person. For example, the old great-grandmother's speech on her birthday, practically every line is something that somebody actually said to us, but it's a composite of many different people. We met a woman who had been the secretary of the agricultural union, and the murder story, the Frank and Val story, was a newspaper cutting abut someone she knew. A lot of the union references in the play were hers. There were a lot of things from one particular woman that went into the character Shirley, who's always working, about pride in working hard and not giving up, lines like 'I didn't want my mother to think she'd bred a gibber.'

We started out very open [about subject matter] — we were going to do a workshop in the Fens. Before we went, Les Waters, the director, and I had talked a lot about people having a bad time in the country: that's where the original sense of direction came from. We made a company of more women than men, so that was a decision affecting the subject of the play that was taken before we began the workshop. We read the book *Fenwomen* by Mary Chamberlain before we went and during the workshop. And by the end of the workshop we had all focused on women land workers and knew the kinds of issues it might be about.

> Churchill, interviewed by Emily Mann, in
> *Interviews with Contemporary Women Playwrights*,
> ed. Kathleen Betsko and Rachel Koenig, p. 80

Midday Sun

Performance art piece.
First London production: ICA, 8 May 1984; transferred
   as Amsterdam, 'Fairground' project, 5 June 1984 (dir. John Ashford,
   Pete Brooks, and Geraldine Pilgrim; choreography Sally Owen;
   lighting Tom Donnellan; sound Graeme Miller; with Seeta Indrani
   and José Nava).

Midday Sun *brings together some of the most inventive talents in a performance art style of theatre, with a writer who has never lacked courage in re-inventing forms. These combined powers, from Impact Theatre and Hesitate and Demonstrate . . . with Caryl Churchill and John Ashford, have produced an event inspired by the experience of voyaging. Morocco is the location and aspects of what Morocco signifies are suggested to our senses. It is explored as the site of our fantasies — nostalgic, sinister and silly — about the exotic. Visual expectation is totally disrupted by awesomely unexpected objects and people. The space, fully lit, becomes a tacky holiday villa and its beach. A tense dialogue draws more conscious attention to how holidays fail our fantasies and to our guilt about the countries we perch in, despite war and deprivation, as tourists. The dialogue is taken further in a passage that becomes an amplified physical and verbal ritual, revealing the hidden sadness and agitation of the words. . . .*

If you're prepared to relinquish the intellectual superiority audiences use in unlikely forms of theatre to gain control over wayward experience, this piece rewards you with pleasure. The pleasures are those of intricate patterns of sound, light and movement which evoke fleeting moods and feelings, and are constructed by Graeme Miller (soundtrack), Tom Donnellan (lighting) and many others with infinite technical patience. It is most powerful when it trusts most to its own means, less when it becomes too anxiously explicit about exploitation of the world's poor.

Susan Todd, 'Territories', *New Statesman*, 18 May 1984

The ideas behind this show are subtle and ingenious; their realization . . . walks a tightrope between the magical and the moribund. It works like this: Caryl Churchill has written a fragment of dialogue for five characters on a Moroccan beach. It's sandwiched between two surreal sequences: Geraldine Pilgrim has imagined the Moroccan scene before it occurs; Pete Brooks has the quintet remember it. The magic includes José Nava swathed in gold bobbing to the strains of Judy Garland; a figure rising mysteriously from a fountain; a radiant set of amber and azure and many tiny shining moments. The problems are that the themes of anticipation and memory are under-exploited so that if you haven't read the blurb, you've no idea what's going on.

Ros Asquith, *City Limits*, 18 May 1984

[The] ideas are worked out with an unhurried obscurity remarkable even at this address. José Nava takes an age to set up mikes for the visitors to mouth, repetitively and often inaudibly over the deafening sound, rationalizations of experience or just private concerns.

The fountain that yields up a drinks tray for Richard Hawley, and disgorges . . . Seeta Indrani like Venus from the shell, finally, like the pull of race or nationality, swallows up the fully-robed Mr. Nava, who then staggers out for a groggy, soggy curtain-call.

Anthony Masters, *The Times*, 10 May 1984

The intention was apt and daring. Ashford recognized that Pilgrim and Brooks, who direct those leading performance art groups, Hesitate and Demonstrate and Impact Theatre, too often failed to provide themselves with the kinds of textual underpinning that their flights of fantasy required. So he brought in the dramatist Caryl Churchill as scriptwriter, and the four of them devised and directed this piece.

Caryl Churchill has, however, provided the other three who also direct the show with a text of quite stupefying banality on which to base their creation, and there are few signs that she or they are quite aware of the base metal which they need to transmute. . . .

Much technique has been put to trivial use.

Nicholas de Jongh, *The Guardian*, 9 May 1984

Softcops

Play in one act.
Written: first draft, 1978; revised 1984.
First London production: by the Royal Shakespeare Company at the Barbican Pit, 2 Jan. 1984 (dir. Howard Davies; des. Bob Crowley; music Nigel Hess; with Geoffrey Freshwater as Vidocq, Malcolm Storry as Lacenaire, and Ian Talbot as Pierre).
Published: London: Methuen, 1984 and in *'Softcops' and 'Fen'*, 1986.

For this premiere production, the Pit's arena-like performance space was draped with white muslin. The Medici String Quartet played among lighted candelabra against a background of discarded paintings, furniture and trunks reminiscent of a forgotten attic. Designer Bob Crowley's basic colours were black and white offset by red ribbons and gloves — the colour of violence, passion, and punishment. The performance style was highly theatrical with twelve actors (all men) playing many parts essentially on a bare stage with few properties. . . .

Churchill focuses on Vidocq . . . and Lacenaire . . . , a cop and robber who, in real life, both wrote memoirs. Vidocq as chief of police uses criminal skills of disguise and cunning. In his cell, Lacenaire, a glamorous and ineffectual murderer and thief, is admired and feted by the wealthy. Two other characters are central to Churchill's thesis. One is Jeremy Bentham . . . , inventor of the panopticon — an iron cage dominated by a tower from which one person is able to watch and control others without being seen — and Pierre . . . , social reformer and softcop who rejects gory punishments and humiliating chain gangs in favour of panopticons and reform schools.

The playwright leads us through the development of softer penal methods and their transformation of the criminal from individual to faceless mob. In the final scene, in which convicts play accompanied by an unarmed warden, Churchill's thesis is complete. While punishment has become softer, it has created no less an abused social class. The Vidocqs and Lacenaires have disappeared from the system.

Milly Barranger, *Theatre Journal*,
XXXVI, 3 (Oct. 1984), p. 418

Softcops is more an animated argument than an act of story-telling. . . . Howard Davies's production is principally a company event, with beautifully choreographed groups merging and dissolving in patterns of robot discipline, mob violence, and waxwork stillness to the crowningly ironic accompaniment of calm philosophic music from the Medici String Quartet.

Irving Wardle, *The Times*, 11 Jan. 1984

The play is more illustrated lecture than drama, though lots of 'dramatic' things happen. . . .

Miss Churchill, I suspect unfortunately, read Michel Foucault's *Surveiller et Punir* and so impressed was she by Foucault's ideas that they have taken over and devoured the play she might have written.

Giles Gordon, *The Spectator*, 21 Jan. 1984

What she's got here are a lot of random notes for a *New Society* article about penal reform but nothing that could remotely be called a play: a lot of RSC talent is being wasted on a show which might just about get by in a lunchtime pub but looks distinctly lost even in the cramped confines of the Barbican basement.

Sheridan Morley, *Punch*, 18 Jan. 1984

We have in Ms. Churchill a writer of great confidence and imagination, and the broad strokes of her theatrical imagery work their usual power. What is lacking is any sense of direction, or indication of authorial viewpoint.

Ned Chaillet, *Wall Street Journal*, 27 Jan. 1984

Caryl Churchill embeds one play inside another around common themes of crime and punishment and learning by example, and makes the audience work very hard indeed for 95 minutes to link the two. The concentration is stimulating but . . . the result remains untypically obscure. . . .

No shortage of ideas, no play.

Michael Radcliffe, *The Observer*, 15 Jan. 1984

So intent is she on stating her message that every whiff of humour is imbued with a grim sense of its sinister implications. Apart from the superb musical accompaniment from the Medici String Quartet, the result is one of the least enjoyable evenings I can remember in three years' regular theatregoing. Enjoyment may not be mandatory, but there are few compensatory factors in *Softcops*; it keeps you guessing, and hoping, but consistently fails to provide what it promises.

Rosalind Carne, *New Statesman*, 27 Jan. 1984

The threat to individual liberty from the card index, the conspiracy of criminal and detective, and finally the sinister pun between social and state security are all revealed before our very eyes. Yet the logic of Foucault's argument seems to be that there is no answer to power and punishment. If there is, Caryl Churchill has not given it.

Robert Hewison, 'A Model Crime', *Sunday Times*, 15 Jan. 1984

Several critics have thus far pointed out that Caryl Churchill's kaleidoscopic survey of crime and punishment offers no solution to the problem. Which is a bit like saying that Torvil and Dean skate pretty figures but are lousy at higher mathematics. The point of the play is to detail the infinite ambiguities surrounding society's need for deterrence and lust for revenge. The result, moving from the blatant barbarism of the thumbscrew to the subtle barbarism of the reformatory, makes it clear that the distinction between old-fashioned sadism and modern enlightenment is a narrow one. Short glittering scenes pile on the effect of a macabrely funny cabaret of cruelty.

Ros Asquith, *City Limits*, 20 Jan. 1984

There are moments when the brimming invention of the art almost overwhelms the matter, but a less frenzied pacing would put this right. I can remember few evenings when theatre and history combined to give such intelligent fun.

Michael Ignatieff, 'A Punishing Routine',
Times Literary Supplement,
20 Jan. 1984, p. 62

The first draft of the play was actually written in 1978, before *Cloud Nine*. It came immediately after a television play called *The Legion Hall Bombing* which was about Northern Ireland and the Diplock courts. That connects up: that play was about the depoliticization of crime, or calling things crimes that other people might call political acts, which is one of the things that *Softcops* is about. I'd been thinking quite a lot in 1977 and 1978 about that and about methods of social control in general. I'd been thinking about how you can control people without the necessity of violent means once you have a whole lot of systems to fit people into. This was of course at the time of the Labour government when it was appropriate to see the government as a 'softcop' (the image being the 'hardcop' who beats you up and the 'softcop' who gives you cups of tea). While I was thinking about all this I read . . . Michel Foucault's book *Discipline and Punish*. . . .

I thought I'm not going to worry about who's going to do this and whether we can do . . . [it] with six people and a chair! In this one we will have crocodiles of schoolchildren, and *mobs*, and *executions* and all the things I know it is completely impractical to have. Then I put it aside and forgot about it until some time later when Howard Davies was approaching me about doing a play for the RSC. . . . He . . . said, yes, finish it. We can have executions, mobs, no problem. . . .

[*Softcops*] shows how hospitals, schools, crime, prisons — things whose existence in their present form one might take for granted — . . . how they're connected . . . and what effects . . . it can have on you that they are like they are. . . . Being free from that control is helped by understanding how it works.

Churchill, interviewed by Lynne Truss,
in *Plays and Players*, Jan. 1984, p. 10

In 1985, as this edition goes to press, the Government are attempting to depoliticize the miners and the rioters by emphasizing 'a criminal element'.

Churchill, Note to the 1986 edition

A Mouthful of Birds

Play in two acts, combining drama and dance.

Written: with David Lan, with choreography by Ian Spink, during
and after a workshop with Joint Stock Theatre Group.

First production: by Joint Stock Theatre Group, first performed at
Birmingham Repertory Th., 29 Aug. 1986, then on tour; first performed in London at the Royal Court Th., 26 Nov. 1986
(dir. Ian Spink and Les Waters; des. Annie Smart; with
Christian Burgess, Dona Croll, Philippe Giraudeau, Stephen Goff,
Tricia Kelly, Vivienne Rochester, and Marjorie Yates, who was
succeeded by Amelda Brown).

Published: London: Methuen, 1986.

---

*Caryl Churchill and David Lan . . . ask us to consider that the
violent forms of ecstasy, possession and violence which
animated Euripides'* The Bacchae *are alive and vigorous in
modern Britain.*

*The play's first scene hints at this association when the
classical figure of Dionysus, a man dressed in long white skirt,
plaits and head-dress, glides swiftly through the two tiers of
Annie Smart's beautiful sinister stage design. It consists of two
tiers of a gutted, bare-walled and dilapidated house, with a
surviving flight of stairs, a Euripidean tree growing up the two
gutted storeys, and a few household objects left intact.*

*Into the midst of this dream-struck territory there come, in
fragmented scenes and sequences, a series of people, seven of
whose lives are disrupted and shattered by the kinds of passion
which ruined Pentheus and his mother Agave. Indeed the
ancient Greek characters flash briefly into the modern British
domesticities. And at the close of part one the company, in one
of choreographer Ian Spink's less impressive dance sequences,
are possessed by the wild Bacchante spirit. And at the piece's
climax the murderous violence of the Bacchae infects and infests
two of the possessed.*

Nicholas de Jongh, *The Guardian,* 29 Nov. 1986

The structure of the play is that there are seven very short scenes which
show what the characters were doing before the extraordinary things
happen to them. The middle section consists of seven main scenes, and

movement pieces. . . . 'The Fruit Ballet' relates to the sensuousness of tearing things up and 'Extreme Happiness' to the feelings of the women on the mountain. At the end there are seven monologues which show what eventually happens to the characters, how they've changed yet further.

> Churchill, interviewed by Geraldine Cousin in
> 'The Common Imagination and the Individual Voice',
> *New Theatre Quarterly*, IV, 13 (Feb. 1988), p. 10

It's one of those experiences that mystifies, perplexes, aggravates and yanks you clean out of the cosy naturalistic narrative rut that passes for so much contemporary drama. Annie Smart's crumbling two-storey forms the backdrop to a journey into the darker recesses of possession, sexuality (of the bi-sexual, cross-dressing kind) and ecstatic pleasure. . . . A heady experiment in the marriage of words and physical movement (on the whole a pretty successful one) handled by a mixed company of actors/dancers with a skill and precision one can only marvel at. Where does straight narrative go after this?

> Carole Woddis, *City Limits,* 4 Dec. 1986

In *A Mouthful of Birds* . . . there are choric sequences . . . in which the company shift startlingly between benign and demonic extremes, or transubstantiate mimetically before we realize what's going on. They mix movement with spoken, intellectually rooted drama more smoothly than I have seen in a long time.

> Jim Hiley, *The Listener*, 4 Dec. 1986

An event that, for all its maddening opacity, is in fact a genuine experimental departure of physical bravery and intellectual validity.

> Michael Coveney, *Financial Times*, 28 Nov. 1986

What counts is not the basic events, but the means by which the production . . . takes you inside the heads of the afflicted characters, either in nightmare or ecstasy, making you feel how easily you could act as they do. . . .

Dance figures prominently in the show. When the victims dance it is a jerky, autistic ballet of imprisonment. Only when the two figures of Dionysus (Philippe Giraudeau and Stephen Goff) take the stage does it expand into the flowing line of those who are at peace with their own bodies.

> Irving Wardle, 'Serious Change of Life',
> *The Times*, 28 Nov. 1986

The trouble is a lack of form. The many individually intriguing fragments were never dismembered from a whole play and they cannot be reconstituted into one. . . .

Like so many improvisation-based efforts, the outcome is jerky and episodic, with mundane natter one moment and frenzied shrieking the next, constantly risking the clichés and bathos which threaten the Method. At the same time, this company of seven is very good at it; all are swiftly and passionately 'possessed' by their roles (and there are quite a lot of lines that are deliberately funny as well).

Oliver Taplin, 'A Surfeit of Ecstasy',
Times Literary Supplement, 12 Dec. 1986, p. 1403

A Mouthful of Birds . . . goes for the darker side of the Dionysian experience. . . .

But strangely, partly because it lifts us out of the humdrum and partly because it uses surprising and visually beautiful means to do so, Caryl Churchill and David Lan's play is a joyful evening. Over all of it is a sly, provocative humour which raises even the grimmest of its scenes of possession; and I felt a tremendous sense of relief at its acknowledgement of our unfriendlier inner voices and demons. . . .

Some of the scenes don't work and there are patches of obscurity. What the play lacks is precisely what the best performance pieces — such as those by Pina Bausch, whom Churchill has cited as an influence, or those of the People Show or some of Natasha Morgan — demonstrate superbly: the stamp of a single person or long-standing group of collaborators over the whole evening, which then flows by an associative logic that seems as inevitable as it is unpredictable. *A Mouthful of Birds* is uneven; its abandon has a willed, gritted-teeth quality to it.

Victoria Radin, *New Statesman*, 5 Dec. 1986

On stage it is easy to miss the cohering point; that after the slaughter the Joint Stock's Bacchae deny the myth and remain on the mountain, refusing to return to the vacuity of sane life. They have learnt the lesson of the characters in the sketches, that there is no peace, only anti-climax, when the Bacchanalia is done.

Alex Renton, *The Independent*, 2 Dec. 1986

A Mouthful of Birds . . . started life in 'the Workshop'. . . . The result of what was doubtless a worthwhile experiment should however have remained in 'the Workshop', and it is surprising that it was allowed out

onto the main house stage of the Royal Court. . . . As we so often hear
these days, productions must be granted the 'right to fail'. This one is a
failure and audiences appear, understandably, to be availing themselves
of the right to an early dinner.

> Christopher Edwards,
> *The Spectator*, 13 Dec. 1986

Which came first, the writing or the dance?

From early on Ian Spink was working on movement ideas thrown up by
The Bacchae ('Fruit Ballet', 'Extreme Happiness'). Meanwhile
David Lan and I came up with the idea of seven characters and wrote
their scenes, indicating in them where there should be dance, which Ian
then made ('Pig', 'Dancing'). So part of the work came originally from
the choreography and part from the writing. Afterwards the whole
structure was put together and combined with specific references to
The Bacchae.

> Churchill, unpublished interview with Linda Fitzsimmons,
> 20 Apr. 1988

We weren't sure at first if . . . [*The Bacchae*] was even going to be in the
play. It would have been possible just to do our seven stories, but . . .
[*The Bacchae*] brought together so many of the things we used in our
stories. The idea of the dead spirits coming back to possess the play was
very appealing. . . .

There's an obvious analogy between the women in *The Bacchae* who
leave Thebes and go off into the mountains and the women of the peace
camp. . . . People . . . project strange things on to them. . . . I was
interested in the danger of polarizing men and women into the
traditional view that men are naturally more violent and so have no
reason to change. It's important to recognize women's capacity for
violence and men's for peace. . . .

People always talk as if they're . . . horrified by violence, they don't
recognize what pleasure there is when there are football crowds . . . or
even, perhaps, nuclear war. . . . There is a . . . pleasure in things being so
terrible and so extreme. You have to recognize it, otherwise you're only
trying to resist it on a rational level which just says this is bad and we
don't want it. Actually it's not as simple as that. It's a thing of using
your strength and power.

> Churchill, interviewed by John Vidal in
> 'Legend of a Woman Possessed',
> *The Guardian*, 21 Nov. 1986

There was a line that David [Lan] and I worked out when we were first thinking about the play. . . . We thought that perhaps, at the beginning of the play, we would have passive, weak, peaceful women and rather angry, violent men. The middle section, the possession stories, would deal with violent women and men who are weakened or sexually more uncertain, and we suddenly realized that this fitted with precisely the kind of people who tend to become possessed in societies where possession is a very common thing.

In the final stages there would be what we were provisionally calling 'women warriors' — by which we meant strong women, but strong in choosing not to be violent — and more peaceable unmacho men. This was terribly schematic, of course, and we didn't keep to it, but there is a feeling of it that runs through the play, and in some of the characters you can see the idea carried through.

> Churchill, interviewed by Geraldine Cousin, as above, p. 10

It's the first time I feel I've really collaborated with another writer. I did like it. I wouldn't want to do it too often. I think it's like the things when you work with a company, you then want to draw back and do something of your own and be clear what's yours and not just response to other people.

> Churchill, unpublished interview with Linda Fitzsimmons,
> 10 Sept. 1987

Serious Money

Play in two acts with, as a curtain-raiser, part of Act II, Scene i,
   of Thomas Shadwell's *The Volunteers; or, The Stockjobbers*, 1692.
Written: after a workshop with the Royal Court Th.
First London production: Royal Court Th., 21 Mar. 1987
   (dir. Max Stafford-Clark; des. Peter Hartwell; songs Ian Dury,
   Micky Gallagher, and Chaz Jankel; with Linda Bassett, Burt Caesar,
   Allan Corduner, Lesley Manville, Alfred Molina, Gary Oldman,
   Meera Syal, Julian Wadham); trans. to Wyndham's Th., 6 July 1987
   (with Linda Bassett, Burt Caesar, Scott Cherry, Allan Corduner,
   Paul Moriarty, Joanne Pearce, Meera Syal, Daniel Webb);
   trans. Joseph Papp's Public Th., New York, 22 Nov. 1987.
First American production: Royale Th., Broadway, New York,
   20 Jan. 1988 (dir. Max Stafford-Clark; with Alec Baldwin,
   Allan Corduner, Cordelia Gonzalez, Melinda Mullins, Kate Nelligan,
   John Pankow, Wendell Pierce, Michael Wincott).
Published: London: Methuen, 1987.

Serious Money . . . *is a socialist play about capitalist pleasure , conjuring up the exhilaration of the chase after millions. And in acknowledging commerce's allure beyond logic, Churchill frees herself to cogitate — albeit with gleeful authenticity — by means of a festive romp.* Serious Money *is a raucous, complex, but sublimely theatrical swim against prevailing tides of thought, which charms not least because the actors — each playing a clutch of roles under Max Stafford-Clark's quick-fire direction — so patently enjoy themselves. What's communicated is a sense of buoyant but informed resistance.*

Framed by busy monitors, banks of telephones and shelves of champagne, the production concocts an environment of bawled deals and schoolboy horseplay, where trysts and even funerals vexatiously slow the gravy train. Here Billy Corman (Gary Oldman), a corporate raider of East End origins, pursues the old North Country firm of Albion with mean-mouthed frenzy. His allies include the single-minded but droll American banker Zackerman (Alfred Molina) and — less reliably — Marylou Baines (Linda Bassett), a Wall Street arbitrageuse 'second only to Boesky'. On to this scene of compulsive bluff and multiple treachery, where Tory oiks are rapidly deposing Conservative gentlemen, arrive Jacinta Condor (Meera Syal), an ambitious Peruvian with a finger in the cocaine trade, . . . and assorted wealth-mongers of dubious allegiance.

Churchill's script — much of it in beguilingly obtrusive rhyme — suggests the codes and minutiae of City culture without ever losing a broad satirical edge. We meet Corman's hangers-on, like the stockbroker, rationalizing her master's nefariousness to suit professional proprieties, and the publicist, who counsels an image of 'sexy greed' for the late 1980s. And we learn that Albion, for all its 'family business' facade, is run on principles as ruthless as Corman's. But with an election brewing, the takeover battle threatens to embarrass the government. As a loyal Conservative, Corman bows to clandestine pressure, later to be rewarded by the inevitable knighthood, not to mention the chairmanship of the National Theatre. His withdrawal from the fray helps secure victory: at the end, one of Ian Dury's pair of scorchingly vulgar songs promises 'Five more glorious years'.

On top of all this, a wonderful plot revolves around the unexplained death of an upper-crust dealer (Julian Wadham), and the efforts of his sister (Lesley Manville) to trace the malefactor. Much is made of the murder's significance, but it fizzles out with a tantalizingly offhand reference to MI5 and the CIA.

Jim Hiley, *The Listener*, 2 Apr. 1987

There are good moments of explanation, and even better ones of musical explosion at the end of each half — both songs have words by Ian Dury, the first an obscenity scat chant for gaudily-jacketed trading oiks, the second a pulsating pub rock hymn to five more glorious years of a Tory Government, concupiscence and ratified pillage.

But Ms. Churchill has spun a thriller narrative through the middle of the dealings and betrayals that is both feeble and muddling. There is a hovering air of what it is that has driven the public school-boy Jake . . . to suicide, but the details are buried in such awkwardly affixed second act developments as the copper mine sales of a Peruvian heiress and the cocaine market manoeuverings of an Eton-educated Nigerian potentate.

Ms. Churchill's technique of wrapping the text up in a versifying melange of Victorian pantomime couplets and second-rate doggerel after the style of Steven Berkoff is a . . . great drawback. Where iambics are used, the scansion is erratic and annoying. And the rhyming of four-letter crudities becomes predictable and uninventive. The idea is to catch the desperate furore and noisiness of the dealers' world, but the text needs much more highlighting and pointing — the overlapping dialogue passages and ensemble 'blah-blahs' are just messy.

Michael Coveney, *Financial Times*, 30 Mar. 1987

Churchill doesn't make the mistake of thinking Corman is any worse than the representatives of older money, whom she shows to be every bit as ruthless; nor of believing that integrity ruled before the Bang released naked greed in its most incontrovertible forms. Her curtain-raising scene lifted from Thomas Shadwell shows Restoration pillars of the establishment merrily dreaming up trading chicaneries and a playwright rejoicing in it. Churchill rejoices in it too; and has a good time at peppering her play with awful puns, rhyming couplets and theatrical in-jokes. . . . I don't think this is a lasting work, but its quality of cheap immediacy, an inky newness like this morning's tabloid, gives it a freshness one rarely sees in the theatre: it feels as if it had been written today.

Victoria Radin, *New Statesman*, 3 Apr. 1987

Perhaps the best compliment one can pay both the cast and playwright is to say that as well as making fun of that world (often wittily), as well as judging it by exaggerating its more grotesque aspects, they also manage to do justice to its quality of awful exhilaration.

Christopher Edwards, *The Spectator*, 11 Apr. 1987

You feel Ms. Churchill, the director, Max Stafford-Clark, and the cast are as fascinated by the City's frenzied energy as they are appalled by its moral unscrupulousness. . . .

Its main thrust is that the new, post-Big Bang City is merely the old writ crude and that the Square Mile is a place where no bad deed goes wholly unrewarded. . . .

The form of the play is also the key to its energy since Ms. Churchill has cast much of it in a rhyming verse that suggests a weird mix of Hilaire Belloc, Cyril Fletcher and provincial panto. Sometimes it is just doggerel: at others it trimly encapsulates a point. . . .

The heartening thing about Max Stafford-Clark's production is that it attacks the City's greed and fear with zest rather than self-righteousness.

Michael Billington, 'Money Talks', *The Guardian*, 30 Mar. 1987

Caryl Churchill's post-Big Bang 'city comedy' is a piece in the great Royal Court tradition: an angry, witty, front-line report on Britain, introducing characters and environments new to the theatre that affect all our lives. It is also staged and cast with high-gloss precision.

Irving Wardle, 'Vigorous Drama of a New Elite',
The Times, 30 Mar. 1987

It is written almost entirely in rhyme. The verse dialogue, handled superbly by the actors, contributes a sense of verbal gymnastics, with the audience almost holding its breath at times to see how an impossible-sounding rhyme will be completed. The driving rhythm of the verse also serves quite effectively to convey the frenetic pace at which life in the City moves, and its restraints suggest the extent to which the supposedly powerful barons of high finance are controlled by the environment in which they operate.

Amelia Howe Kritzer, '*Serious Money*',
Theatre Journal, XXXIV, 3 (Oct. 1987), p. 394-5

Murder provides a ricketty peg to hang a rambling plot (forget it — the author does), and a pretext to display what should evidently be a parade of Grosz-like caricatures but which ends up a slag-heap of stereotypes.

References are self-consciously rammed in ('The International Tin Council — what a scandal!' cries one character directly to the audience to let us know how much homework has been done). The witless if facetious writing is churned out in doggerel, neither Restoration couplets nor Victorian panto poesy but a broken-backed jumble of varying rhythms, metre and rhyme that the author shoves into the ragbag from one moment to the next. . . .

Insiders may well enjoy the play. Outsiders may experience a numbing boredom.

Martin Hoyle, *Financial Times*, 7 July 1987

Designed by Ms. Churchill as a savage attack on the City, the same rough-edged dealers have flocked to see it in their hundreds, organizing parties, taking the whole office, and having fun identifying themselves on the stage.

Neil Collins, *Daily Telegraph*, 8 July 1987

It's now a bit like going to see *The Resistible Rise of Arturo Ui* with a coach party of SS men.

Thomas Sutcliffe, *The Independent*, 15 July 1987

If you capture accurately enough the world of the people you are depicting, then it's very flattering and they will come and see it, just as people did in the Restoration.

Max Stafford-Clark, quoted by Michael M. Thomas,
'City Slickers', *Vanity Fair*, Dec. 1987, p. 76

I don't share the mystification of some as to why City audiences flock to see themselves pilloried; in modern life, with its thirst for extrinsic gifts of public image and identity, any attention is better than none. And let us not forget that *Serious Money* depicts a world in which sheer barbarism is an attribute much prized, at least when it comes to getting the sharp deal done. . . . What once no normally brought-up person would have liked to see in his psychological mirror is now — in the City and on Wall Street — cause for admiration.

Michael M. Thomas, as above, p. 76

It's easy to see why this play was such a big hit in London. . . . It combines the spectacle of actors misbehaving (using bad language, pulling down one another's trousers, pretending to vomit, or simulating defecating horses) with a confirmation of many of the British intelligentsia's most dearly held beliefs: that privatization and free enterprise are bad things, that 'the British Empire was a cartel', that foreigners buy Burberrys, that money is somehow something that one is better off yearning for than having, and that while various hidden vices may be permitted in good society, open ambition is unpleasant and impolite. I don't think American audiences are so likely to be snowed by Miss Churchill's play. I think it will be pretty clear to everyone that the satire is rather tame and serves to glamorize rather than to ridicule the world of high finance, by making money look sexy and exciting — which, of course, it is. In fact, I think it will be pretty clear to most people that Caryl Churchill and the Royal Court Theatre (and, by extension, the Public Theatre) are cashing in on 'eighties ethics and yuppie fashion. . . .

It's salutary, I think, to see first-rate acting of a sort that the American stage tradition provides no basis for; also to learn how very little it takes to impress the British politically.

Mimi Kramer, 'Business as Usual', *The New Yorker*, 14 Dec. 1987

What happened in the workshop period?

The suggestion came from Max to do a play about the City. He'd been thinking about it for years. The timing was very lucky.

The workshop was two weeks long. We went down to the City and met people. It was a number of actors, me and Max, Philip Palmer who was the literary manager at the Court, Mark Long from the People Show, and Colin Sell who is the musical director of the play. We would go to the viewing galleries and watch how the different markets worked and get talking to people and, when we could, get taken down to the floor, and follow up any other contacts we had. After that two weeks I did more research all through the autumn and didn't start writing it until after Christmas. We started rehearsals on 15 February and so I left the writing very late.

What form did the research take?

I went back to some of the people we'd seen before and spent some time sitting in dealing rooms hearing what people say. And reading books and the *Financial Times*. There were days when it seemed I did nothing except sit surrounded by newspapers, cutting bits out and sticking them in scrapbooks.

How closely did Ian Dury work with you in writing the songs?

For the first song he came to see the LIFFE scene and I gave him a list of phrases that are used by dealers. For the second one I said that we wanted it to be a celebration of the Conservative Party victory — and again included a few possible phrases, like 'five more glorious years' which was already in the play.

Churchill, unpublished interview with Linda Fitzsimmons,
10 Sept. 1987

I heard that Benjamin Zephania (the black poet) was writing a play, and thought how much I would enjoy the play in verse that I imagined him writing. Then I thought how much more I would enjoy writing my play if it were in verse.

Churchill, unpublished interview with Linda Fitzsimmons,
21 Apr. 1988

[Did you write it in verse] because you wanted to give yourself an extra discipline or did you think it particularly appropriate?

No, I thought it was hard enough without imposing discipline. I think it was two things: I think it was partly the slightly documentary nature of the material, or what I feared might be the dryness of the material (although actually it isn't dry at all), and thinking that it would give it a theatrical edge. . . . More important, it was a way of catching the energy and wit of that world. And it does have the effect of driving the play incredibly fast which seems very right for it.

Churchill, interviewed by Jenni Murray on *P.M.*,
BBC Radio 4, 21 Mar. 1987

The huge energy was something that impressed us and that we wanted to capture. . . . I think a thing that does happen is that people confuse attractiveness and goodness. . . . We wanted to create that paradox in the play — that tension between it being an attractive world and a dangerous one.

Churchill, interviewed by Geraldine Cousin, in
'The Common Imagination and the Individual Voice',
New Theatre Quarterly, IV, 13 (Feb. 1988), p. 16

Fugue

Twenty-four minute play with dance.
Transmitted: Channel 4, *Dancelines*, 26 June 1988 (dir. and
    chor. Ian Spink; des. Antony McDonald; with Lucy Burge,
    Philippe Giraudeau, Stephen Goff, Sally Owen, Josephine Parker
    and Sebastian Shaw).

Narrative and dance show the effect of death on a family, reflecting the circumstances of Bach's funeral, danced to Bach's Contrapunctus 10 from the Art of Fugue.

On New Forms

Playwrights don't give answers, they ask questions. We need to find new questions, which may help us to answer the old ones or make them unimportant, and this means new subjects and new form. . . . What is said and how it's said are hardly separable in the theatre; setting, language and form are all part of the way of looking of a play. So that if the range of theatre is to be widened this will come partly from greater technical range, from the ability to use the medium more fully.

'Not Ordinary, Not Safe', *The Twentieth Century*,
Nov. 1960, p. 448

On Radio Plays

[I went on writing short plays for radio] partly because [I liked radio but also because] I began having children. . . . There was also a better market for them. It was very different, in the early 'sixties. There wasn't anywhere near the number of fringe and lunchtime theatres, and the radio was an accessible way of having your plays done. . . . If your play was seventeen minutes long, they wouldn't ask you to make it thirteen.

Interview with Judith Thurman,
'Caryl Churchill: the Playwright Who Makes You Laugh',
Ms, May 1982, p. 54

[In the radio plays] I focused on the awfulness of everything, rather than on the possibilities for change.

Interview with Judith Thurman, as above, p. 54

Radio is good because it makes you . . . precise. . . . Then there's the freedom — you can do almost anything in a radio play, whereas you're tied to the possibilities of the set and the stage in the theatre. I think in those days I was more concerned with words, and less with events, though . . . I feel I'm better at managing events now. . . .

I . . . reached the point of finding it hard to make people speak to each other — there would simply be monologues delivered, say, by one twin and then the other. I felt this . . . Becketty thing happening: . . . I was going to finish up with a play that was two words and a long silence. Then things began

3: The Writer on Her Work

85

to get better. These plays weren't necessarily depressing: some were fairly funny, but they had to do in some way with difficulties of being.

Interview with John Hall in 'Close Up', *The Guardian*, 12 Dec. 1972

On Television Plays

I don't think I've written a play for television yet which is a really deeply considered play like the plays I've written for the stage. The best one isn't a play at all, which is the adaptation of the Legion Hall Bombing, which is an adaptation of a trial.

Unpublished interview with Linda Fitzsimmons, 10 Sept. 1987

On Playtexts as Blueprints

Do you continue to be involved in subsequent productions of your plays?

I alternate between being very involved where I am involved, like in the first production, and letting it go when it's gone, because I don't know what else you can do with a play.

A playtext is like a blueprint which you can do different ways, so you don't go expecting it to be the same. And then sometimes what people have discovered you like and sometimes you don't. It's sometimes a pleasant surprise and sometimes not.

Unpublished interview with Linda Fitzsimmons, as above

On Working with Joint Stock

In 1976 I started writing for fringe companies, which I suddenly found a lot more attractive [than the Royal Court]. I wanted to work with touring companies, and with people who had more political interests, and in workshops. . . . It's a matter of having a director and actors with whom you can share certain assumptions and not have to feel that you are constantly the one to be trying to push things in the direction you want them to go.

Unpublished transcript of symposium held in 1981 at Louisiana State University, Baton Rouge: *Playwrights at the Royal Court Theatre, 1956-1981: a Discussion by Representative 'Court' Writers,* ed. Gresdna A. Doty and Billy J. Harbin

The only workshop things I've ever done have been those four Joint Stock shows and *Serious Money*. There's a common misapprehension that all of my work is from workshops. The other misapprehension, of course, is that doing a workshop play means that it's improvised and you've just written down what the actors have said.

> Unpublished interview with Linda Fitzsimmons, as above

When you've worked closely with companies you must have had to be fairly accommodating to other people's ideas?

[Sometimes] I'll be extremely open in rehearsal — if someone says, can we move this speech to the end, I'll say . . . fine let's try [it]. . . . Other times I will find myself being . . . pernickity and saying 'Look, you're saying "Well", and there isn't one', or 'you've got a word wrong'. For me it actually throws out the whole rhythm and point of the line. At that point I can be very uncompromising.

> Interview with Lynne Truss, 'A Fair Cop',
> *Plays and Players*, Jan. 1984, p. 9

What are the advantages of the workshop method?

The actual writing time is obviously fairly short, but to have the long rehearsals, to be able to work with actors for that amount of time is very nice. You have to keep that balance between keeping your own ideas quite clear and strong and being open at the same time. The advantage of not doing a workshop is not to have to do that and just to be able to do what you want. Not to have to be open, I think, it's quite nice sometimes just to be able to do that.

> Unpublished interview with Linda Fitzsimmons, as above

I like [collaboration]. I'd always been very solitary as a writer before and I like working that closely with other people. [With Joint Stock] you don't collaborate on writing the play, you still go away and write it yourself, so that to that extent it's the same as usual. What's different is that you've had a period of researching something together, not just information, but your attitudes to it, and possible ways of showing things, which means that when you come back with the writing you're much more open to suggestions.

> Interview with Kathleen Betsko and Rachel Koenig,
> *Interviews with Contemporary Women Playwrights*, p. 79

If you're working by yourself, then you're not accountable to anyone but yourself while you're doing it. You don't get forced in quite the same way into seeing how your own inner feelings connect up with larger things that happen to other people. If you're working with a group of people, one approach is going to have to be from what actually happened or what everyone knows about — something that exists outside oneself.

Did you have a clear idea by the end of [each] workshop period of the play you wanted to write?

Each time I've started writing a completely different play and scrapped it some way through the writing period. It's interesting because the plays seem to come very obviously from the workshops, but the workshops were so rich in material that you could write dozens of different plays and they'd all be relevant. I have seemed to need each time to get a greater distance, a second lot of digestion, between me and the workshop.

Interview with Geraldine Cousin, 'The Common Imagination and the Individual Voice', *New Theatre Quarterly*, IV, 13 (Feb. 1988), p. 4, 6

On Working with Max Stafford-Clark

I work very well with Max Stafford-Clark. He is very good at suggesting cuts and revisions, and I . . . have a say about the way in which I think the text should be presented on the stage. And so the version which we eventually recognize as the definitive one is often reached at a very late stage.

Interview with Maggie Rose, in 'A Woman's Point of View', *Sipario*, Nov.-Dec. 1987, p. 100

On Political Theatre

Does the playwright have an obligation to take a moral and political stance?

It's almost impossible not to take one, whether you intend to or not. Most plays can be looked at from a political perspective and have said something, even if it isn't what you set out to say. If you wrote a West End comedy relying on conventional sexist jokes, that's taking a moral and political stance, though the person who wrote it might say, 'I was just writing an entertaining show.' Whatever you do your point of view is going to show somewhere. It usually only gets noticed and called 'political' if it's against the status quo. There are times when I feel I want to deal with immediate issues and times when I don't. I do like the stuff of theatre, in the same way that people who are painting like paint; and of course when you say 'moral and political' that doesn't have to imply reaching people logically or overtly, because theatre can reach people on all kinds of other levels too. . . . Sometimes it's going to be about images, more like a dream to people, and sometimes it's going to be more like reading an article.

Interview with Kathleen Betsko and Rachel Koenig, as above, p. 79-80

I've constantly said that I am both a socialist and a feminist. Constantly said it. If someone says 'a socialist playwright' or 'a feminist playwright' that can suggest to some people something rather narrow which doesn't cover as many things as you might be thinking about. I get asked if I mind being called a woman playwright or a feminist playwright, and again it depends entirely on what's going on in the mind of the person who says it.

Unpublished interview with Linda Fitzsimmons, 21 Apr. 1988

On Women Playwrights

Are you conscious of exploring different gender-based ideas at any one particular time?

I think originally I wasn't really interested in gender ideas at all. I probably made men main characters without thinking of it consciously . . . but just because main characters tended to *be* men. It was also perhaps easier to conceive of characters separate from myself by making them men. . . . [I was reacting against the] semi-autobiographical novels that quite a lot of women of my generation were starting to write — Françoise Sagan, for example, and Margaret Drabble. . . . I wanted to make something more distanced. . . . [Later] I became increasingly interested in women's issues and consciously chose to write about those.

Do you think of yourself not just as a writer, but as a 'woman writer'?

Sometimes. Originally, not. During the 'seventies there was a context for thinking of myself as a woman writer. . . . If . . . a critic refers to you as one of the best women writers, and you feel there's any possibility that he thinks of that as a *lesser* category, you resent the use of it as a term. If it means women themselves thinking about things that they haven't thought about before, then you can actually feel very positive about the idea of being a woman writer, and obviously this is attractive and powerful. Most of the time I don't think about it either way, really.

Interview with Geraldine Cousin, as above, p. 5

Is there a female aesthetic?

I don't see how you can tell until there are so many plays by women that you can begin to see what they have in common that's different from the way men have written, and there are still relatively so few. I . . . remember before I wrote *Top Girls* thinking about women barristers — how they were in a minority and had to imitate men to succeed — and I was thinking of them as different from me. And then I thought, 'Wait a minute, my whole concept of what plays might be is from plays written by men. I don't have to put on a wig, speak in a special voice, but how far do I assume things that have been defined by men?' There isn't a simple answer to that. And I remember long before that thinking of the 'maleness' of the traditional structure of plays, with conflict and building in a certain way to a climax. But it's not something I think about very often. Playwriting will change not just because more women are doing it but because more women are doing other things as well. . . .

Most theatres are still controlled by men and people do tend to be able to see promise in people who are like themselves. . . . If you are at the stage where you are promising but not doing it all that well yet, it's perhaps easier for a man choosing plays to see the potential in a man writer. . . . People don't usually start out writing masterpieces and women may have less chance of getting started. Having productions does seem to make people write better.

Has the political climate for women dramatists changed drastically since you began writing plays?

I began writing plays in 1958, and I don't think I knew of any other women playwrights then. Luckily, I didn't think about it. . . .[Tillie Olsen in *Silences*] says that at different times, whole categories of people are enabled to write. You tend to think of your own development only having to do with yourself and it's exciting to discover it in a historical context.

Interview with Kathleen Betsko and Rachel Koenig, as above, p. 76-7

Women are traditionally expected not to initiate action, and plays are action, in a way that words are not. So perhaps that's one reason why comparatively few women have written plays.

Unpublished interview with Linda Fitzsimmons, 21 Apr. 1988

On Writing Comedy

How much do you aim for comic effects?

I don't think I set out to be funny. Things that end up being serious or being funny I usually set about in exactly the same way. And it isn't really clear which it's going to be until I'm quite far on into the material.

Interview with Lynne Truss, as above, p. 9

On Interviews

I don't really like being interviewed very much. I dislike the feeling of being pinned down as being one thing or another, a feeling that that definition is perhaps limiting what people expect of you.

I don't think things you say in interviews necessarily reflect your work. What I find I do — I'm beginning to learn not to — I think I tend to respond to the questions asked as if I believed there was a correct answer which I don't quite know, and will I be able to come up with it. And another thing: whenever I read them, they're nearly always misquotes anyway. So that I have given up thinking of them as reflecting anything about me. The amount of stuff that's down in quotation marks as me having said, that I know I've never said at all. So that it's all pointless really.

Unpublished interview with Linda Fitzsimmons, 10 Sept. 1987

a: Primary Sources

Collections

Plays: One, with introductions to each play. London: Methuen, 1985. [*Owners, Traps, Vinegar Tom, Light Shining in Buckinghamshire, Cloud Nine.*]
'Softcops' and 'Fen'. London: Methuen, 1986.

Articles and Essays

"Not Ordinary, Not Safe', *The Twentieth Century*, Nov. 1960, p. 443-51.
'Fear and Loathing in the City', *City Limits*, 16 July 1987, p. 12-13.
'Driven by Greed and Fear', *New Statesman*, 17 July 1987, p. 10-11.

Interviews

The Guardian, 12 Dec. 1972, with John Hall.
Sunday Telegraph, 17 Dec. 1972, with Frank Marcus.
Plays and Players, Jan. 1973, with Steve Gooch.
Time Out, 21-27 Oct. 1977, with Ann McFerran.
Sunday Times Magazine, 2 Mar. 1980, with Ronald Hayman.
Radio Times, 10-16 Apr. 1982, with Jeananne Crowley.
The Observer, 15 Aug. 1982, with Victoria Radin.
The Daily Telegraph, 21 Feb. 1983, with John Barber.
The Village Voice, 1 Mar. 1983, with Laurie Stone.
Vogue, Aug. 1983, with John Simon.
Theater Heute, Jan. 1984, with Renate Klett.
Plays and Players, Jan. 1984, with Lynne Truss.
The Guardian, 21 Nov. 1986, with John Vidal.
Interviews with Contemporary Women Playwrights, ed. Kathleen Betsko and Rachel Koenig (New York: Beech Tree Books, 1987), with Betsko and Koenig, and Emily Mann.
Sipario, Nov.-Dec. 1987, with Maggie Rose.
New Theatre Quarterly, IV, 13 (Feb. 1988), with Geraldine Cousin.

b: Secondary Sources

John F. O'Malley, *Caryl Churchill, David Mercer, and Tom Stoppard: a Study of Contemporary British Dramatists who have Written for Radio, Television, and Stage.* Unpublished dissertation, Florida State University, 1974.

Ann McFerran, 'Fringe Beneficiaries', *Time Out*, Sept. 1976, p. 10-11. [On Joint Stock workshop on *Light Shining in Buckinghamshire*.]

Gillian Hanna, 'Feminism and Theatre', *Theatre Papers*, Second Series, No. 8 (1978), p. 9-10. [On *Vinegar Tom*.]

Michelene Wandor, 'Free Collective Bargaining', *Time Out*, 30 Mar.-4 Apr., 1979, p. 14-16. [On Joint Stock workshop on *Cloud Nine*.]

Catherine Itzin, *Stages in the Revolution.* London: Methuen, 1980, p. 279-87. [Interview and comment on some of the radio plays, *The Legion Hall Bombing* (including the original prologue and epilogue and the BBC's prologue) and the major stage plays up to *Cloud Nine*.]

Christian W. Thomsen, 'Three Socialist Playwrights: John McGrath, Caryl Churchill, Trevor Griffiths', *Contemporary English Drama*, Stratford-upon-Avon Studies 19, ed. C.W.E. Bigsby. London: Edward Arnold, 1981, p. 157-75. [On *Owners, Vinegar Tom, Light Shining in Buckinghamshire, Traps* and *Cloud Nine*.]

Alisa Solomon, 'Witches, Ranters and the Middle Class: The Plays of Caryl Churchill', *Theater*, XII, 2 (Spring 1981), p. 49-55. [On *Owners, Vinegar Tom, Light Shining in Buckinghamshire* and *Traps*.]

Gresdna A. Doty and Billy J. Harbin, eds., *Playwrights at the Royal Court Theatre, 1956-1981: a Discussion by Representative 'Court' Writers.* Unpublished transcript of symposium held at Louisiana State University, Baton Rouge, Fall 1981.

Judith Thurman, 'Caryl Churchill: the Playwright Who Makes You Laugh about Orgasm, Racism, Class Struggle, Homophobia, Woman-Hating, the British Empire, and the Irrepressible Strangeness of the Human Heart', *Ms*, May 1982, p. 52-7.

Ruby Cohn, 'Modest Proposals of Modern Socialists', *Modern Drama*, XXV, 4 (Dec. 1982), p. 457-68. [On *Cloud Nine*.]

Helene Keyssar, 'The Dramas of Caryl Churchill — the Politics of Possibility', *The Massachusetts Review*, XXIV, 1 (Spring 1983), p. 198-216. [Reprinted in slightly revised version in Helene Keyssar, *Feminist Theatre* (London and Basingstoke: Macmillan, 1984), p. 77-101. On the major stage plays from *Owners* to *Top Girls*.]

Michael Merschmeier, 'Viktoria, Victoria?', *Theater Heute*, Jan. 1983, p. 32-3. [Review of German premiere of *Cloud Nine*, Schlosspark-theater, Berlin.]

Laurie Stone, 'Caryl Churchill: Making Room at the Top', *The Village Voice*, XXVIII, 9 (1 Mar. 1983), p. 1, 80-1. [Interview and critical comment, mostly on *Top Girls*.]

Michelene Wandor, 'The Fifth Column: Feminism and Theatre', *Drama*, No. 152 (1984), p. 7. [On *Cloud Nine*.]

Mariangela Tempera, 'Il rapporto autore/spettatore nel teatro di memoria colletiva: Peter Nichols, Arnold Wesker, Caryl Churchill', *Quaderni di Filologia Germanica*, III (1984), p. 267-79.

Renate Klett and Reinhardt Stumm, 'Autorenportrait: Caryl Churchill', *Theater Heute*, Jan. 1984, p. 19-27. [Interview, comment, reviews of various German productions of *Top Girls*, including the German premiere at Cologne, referred to by Churchill in Betsko and Koenig as 'a complete travesty'.]

Sue-Ellen Case and Jeanie K. Forte, 'From Formalism to Feminism', *Theater*, XVI, 2 (Spring 1985), p. 62-5. [On *Cloud Nine*.]

Elin Diamond, 'Refusing the Romanticism of Identity: Narrative Interventions in Churchill, Benmussa, Duras', *Theatre Journal*, XXXVII, 3 (Oct. 1985), p. 273-86. [On *Cloud Nine*.]

Vivian M. Patraka, 'Foodtalk in the Plays of Caryl Churchill and Joan Schenkar', *Theater Annual*, XL (1985), p. 137-57. [On *Top Girls* and *Fen*.]

Mark Bly, 'Dramaturgy at the Eureka: an Interview with Oskar Eustis', *Theater*, XVII, 3 (Summer-Fall 1986), p. 11-12. [On *Top Girls* at the Eureka, San Francisco, 1985, dir. Susan Marsden.]

Helene Keyssar, 'Hauntings: Gender and Drama in Contemporary English Theatre', *Englisch Amerikanische Studien*, No. 3-4, (1986), p. 449-68. [On *Vinegar Tom*, *Cloud Nine*, *Top Girls* and *Fen*.]

Michelene Wandor, *Carry On, Understudies: Theatre and Sexual Politics*. London: Routledge and Kegan Paul, 1986, p. 167-74. (First ed., *Understudies: Theatre and Sexual Politics* (London: Methuen, 1981), p. 66-8). [On the major stage plays from *Owners* to *Softcops*, excluding *Fen*.]

Janelle Reinelt, 'Beyond Brecht: Britain's New Feminist Drama', *Theatre Journal*, XXXVIII, 2 (May 1986), p. 154-63. [On *Vinegar Tom*.]

Michael Swanson, 'Mother/Daughter Relationships in Three Plays by Caryl Churchill', *Theatre Studies*, No. 31-32 (1984-6), p. 49-66. [On *Cloud Nine*, *Top Girls* and *Fen*.]

Rob Ritchie, ed., *The Joint Stock Book: the Making of a Theatre Collective*. London: Methuen, 1987, p. 118-21, 138-42, 150-52. [On workshops and rehearsals for *Light Shining in Buckinghamshire*, *Cloud Nine* and *Fen*.]

Michelene Wandor, 'Existential Women: *Owners* and *Top Girls* by Caryl Churchill', *Look Back in Gender: Sexuality and the Family in*

Post-War British Drama. London: Methuen, 1987, p. 119-25.

Joseph Marohl, 'De-realized Women: Performance and Identity in *Top Girls*', *Modern Drama*, XXX, 3 (Sept. 1987), p. 376-88.

Susan Carlson, 'Comic Collisions: Convention, Rage and Order', *New Theatre Quarterly*, III, 12 (Nov. 1987), p. 303-16. [On Griffiths, Barnes, Hayes and *Cloud Nine*.]

Linda Fitzsimmons, ' "I Won't Turn back for You or Anyone": Caryl Churchill's Socialist-Feminist Theatre', *Essays in Theatre*, VI, 1 (Nov. 1987), p. 19-29. [On *Top Girls* and *Fen*.]

Mel Gussow, 'Genteel Playwright, Angry Voice', *The New York Times*, 22 Nov. 1987, p. 1, 26. [On *Serious Money*, including some interview material.]

Michael M. Thomas, 'City Slickers', *Vanity Fair*, Dec. 1987, p. 76-85. [On *Serious Money*.]

Sue-Ellen Case, *Feminism and Theatre*. Basingstoke: Macmillan, 1988. [Brief discussion of *Vinegar Tom*, *Cloud Nine* and *Top Girls*.]

Amelia Howe Kritzer, *Open-Ended Inquiries: the Plays of Caryl Churchill*. Unpublished dissertation, University of Wisconsin-Madison, 1988.

Elin Diamond, '(In)Visible Bodies in Churchill's Theatre', *Theatre Journal*, XL, 2 (May 1988), p. 188-204. [Mainly on *Fen* and *A Mouthful of Birds*.]

Geraldine Cousin, *Churchill: the Playwright*. London: Methuen, forthcoming.

Phyllis Randall, ed., *Caryl Churchill: a Casebook*. New York: Garland, forthcoming. [Includes essays on *A Mouthful of Birds* and *Serious Money*.]

DATE DUE
